READER'S DIGEST BASIC GUIDE
INDOOR GARDENING

Contents

THE TEXT AND ILLUSTRATIONS IN THIS BOOK ARE TAKEN FROM 'READER'S DIGEST ILLUSTRATED GUIDE TO GARDENING' PUBLISHED BY THE READER'S DIGEST ASSOCIATION LIMITED LONDON NEW YORK CAPE TOWN MONTREAL SYDNEY

MONSTERA DELICIOSA

The secret of growing house plants is to give each one the right conditions of light, heat and humidity. So choose the right plants for each part of the house

During the past 20 years house plants have increased enormously in popularity, partly because homes today provide better conditions for indoor plants, and partly because there is now a much greater range of plants available for every situation.

With the introduction of central heating, better insulation and large picture windows, many more colourful and interesting plants can be grown in the home. These range from hardy and easily grown hederas (ivy) and philodendrons, through more exacting plants such as dizygothecas and peperomias, to the difficult group which includes the red-flowered anthuriums and the popular but sensitive saintpaulias (African violet).

Types of house plants

Broadly speaking, house plants fall into two main categories: foliage plants and flowering plants (including flowering pot plants). Foliage plants are either green-leaved or variegated, often with strong, dominating colours. The green-leaved plants are the hardier, and therefore easier to grow, although there are some exceptions, such as adiantums (maidenhair fern) and some of the varieties of ficus (rubber plant).

Coloured foliage plants often need higher temperatures and more humid conditions, which may be difficult to maintain in the home. Calatheas and marantas, which have brilliantly coloured leaves, may fail after a few months, unless their exact growing conditions can be met. On the other hand, the Rex begonias, with their distinctive and colourful leaf markings, and the silvery-banded, purple-backed zebrinas are easily grown.

Variegated leaf plants – chlorophytums, sansevierias, peperomias and tradescantias – are mainly as easy to grow as green foliage plants, but they require a position with better light.

Flowering house plants, such as aphelandras, anthuriums and impatiens (busy lizzie), will flower indoors year after year under the correct conditions, which include annual repotting. Some plants, such as cyclamens and *Euphorbia pulcherrima* (poinsettia), are sometimes difficult to keep from year to year usually because they are brought straight into a living-room that is too warm and dry while they are in flower. They are then often overwatered and neglected when the flowers have finished.

Bromeliads are a special type of plant, grown as much for their unusual foliage as for their flowers. Aechmeas (urn plant), for example, have grey-green leaves and a rose-pink flower spike. In their natural environment, many bromeliads grow on tree trunks, where their roots absorb nourishment from the leaf-mould and other debris which collects there. They therefore need a different compost from other house plants, usually one consisting of peat and sphagnum moss, kept barely moist. Watering is given by topping up the 'vase' formed by the leaves in the centre of the plant.

Flowering pot plants are garden or greenhouse plants that have been specially grown to flower indoors, chiefly in winter and spring. They are sold when the buds have formed, and may flower for several weeks. They need no special care beyond watering, removing dead flowers and providing a suitable atmosphere. Chrysanthemums, calceolarias and azaleas are the most popular indoor-flowering pot plants, but once they have finished blooming they must either be discarded or planted out in a greenhouse border or, if they are hardy, in the garden.

Shape is a factor to be considered in selecting house plants. They may be erect like *Ficus elastica* (rubber plant) or climbing like *Cissus antarctica* (kangaroo vine), both of which will eventually grow to a height of 6 ft or more. Others, like pileas and peperomias, are small and bushy. Tradescantias and zebrinas are trailing, requiring little headroom, but plenty of space to display their drooping stems.

Bear in mind the eventual height and shape of the plant, as well as the climatic atmosphere of each of the rooms, when choosing plants.

Selecting the right plants

Plants are rarely successful if you try adapting them to your home. It is far better to choose plants that will thrive naturally in the rooms where you intend to grow them. Central heating, which provides almost constant warmth, nevertheless has its drawbacks. If it is controlled by a time switch, the contrast between night and day temperatures may be too great – in fact, a drop during the night of more than 8°C (15°F) may slow down the growth of the more delicate plants.

Central heating also creates a dry atmosphere which is harmful to some indoor plants, and in particular to tropical and semi-tropical plants which need a high degree of humidity. Humidity can be increased by setting the plants in trays of damp peat or in saucers of water.

All plants need freely circulating air, but few will tolerate cold draughts. Their growth may slow right down and they may die. Fumes from coal fires, oil and coal gas, can also be damaging, but plants are not affected by natural-gas fumes.

Well-lit areas, such as living-rooms and bedrooms, will suit most house plants provided they are given reasonably humid conditions. South and west-facing rooms provide the best light. Direct sun, however, is not recommended – it should be filtered through net curtains or venetian blinds. During the hottest parts of the day, plants near south-facing windows may need to be moved away from the glass to avoid scorching and wilting.

Unless the window is insulated with double-glazing or heavy curtains the plants should be moved into the room during winter nights, even in centrally heated homes, because of the drop in temperature close to the glass. Do not leave plants in the space between glass and curtains at night.

Plants needing a degree of humidity, such as saintpaulias (African violet) and many of the indoor ferns, do particularly well in warm, moist rooms such as bathrooms and kitchens, provided the day and night temperature variations are not too extreme.

Even for badly lit, draughty places such as stairs and landings, there is a good choice of house plants. Most hederas (ivy), aspidistras, fatsias, fatshederas and several of the philodendrons do extremely well in such conditions.

For the best results, select your house plants according to the requirements you can provide in your home.

Difficult house plants do not thrive in homes without central heating, because of the cooler conditions or bigger variation in temperatures, but both the intermediate and easy groups are perfectly suitable for houses without central heating.

Arranging and grouping plants

Many foliage house plants are seen to their advantage when several are grouped together. Very tall plants, such as *Cissus antarctica*, fatsias, ficus and hederas, are best on their own, for they may dwarf their companions. Rosette-shaped and bushy plants with vivid foliage, as well as flowering pot plants, are also best displayed on their own.

Fast-growing climbers are ideal against room-dividers and bare walls. Many trailing plants, such as tradescantias, zebrinas and *Pelargonium peltatum*, are suitable for hanging on walls – but if possible they should be removed from their wall supports when being watered.

Many florists sell ready-grouped arrangements of three or four plants. They have been removed from their pots and set in a deep container, in a compost of loam, peat and sand with a little added charcoal to prevent the compost going sour.

Such a grouping should include plants that contrast in colour and shape, but they must all have the identical cultural requirements. Tall, erect plants should be kept to the rear, bushy and spreading ones in the centre, and trailing plants to the front of the container. Alternatively, a number of plants, in their pots, can be grouped together in a shallow tray. Stand the pots on pebbles in the tray and pour water between the pebbles for extra humidity.

Plant troughs are ideal for the grouping of foliage plants. They are made from wood, metal, plastic or pottery, and may be free-standing, supported by legs, or ordered to fit an indoor window-sill.

An additional advantage of a plant trough is that it can easily be moved away from too strong a light, or cold windows, to a more shaded or warmer position. Set the pots closely together in the trough to obtain the best contrast or harmony in height, shape, colour, texture and growth habit. The pots can easily be changed around and a few flowering house plants will give additional colour.

The atmosphere immediately around the plants can be kept more moist than that of the room generally, by standing all the pots on pebbles in saucers of water or, ideally, sinking them in moist peat.

Buy plants that will thrive naturally in the position you intend to grow them. The amount of light or shade a plant requires, and its tolerance to draughts or fumes, varies from plant to plant. Plants with thick, dark foliage will tolerate shade; those with variegated leaves need more light. Few plants do well in a draught.

Repotting pot-bound plants

All house plants need to be repotted if they become pot-bound. This happens when a plant has filled its pot with roots and has exhausted the soil in which it is growing.

You can easily tell a pot-bound plant: it makes little or no new growth, and it dries out quickly even after frequent watering. Sometimes the roots penetrate through the drainage holes in the bottom.

Generally, young plants should be repotted into larger pots once a year, in spring or early summer.

Established plants need repotting less frequently, every two to three years or even longer. They can usually be repotted in the same-size pot, with fresh compost.

Because of their confined space, pot-grown plants require more attention to soil, water and light than plants grown in the open. The soil – or compost – must contain the right proportions of essential plant foods: nitrogen, potash and phosphate. It should be free of pests and diseases and sterilised before use. This is a lengthy process, but many ready-mixed, sterilised composts are available.

The John Innes potting composts come in three grades, each consisting of the same proportions of loam, peat and sand, with added fertilisers. No. 3 contains three times as much fertiliser as No. 1.

Other suitable composts include the comparatively new soil-less or loamless composts, sold under brand names. They are largely of peat with fertilisers, and added sand for drainage.

All soil-less composts are suitable for growing house plants; alternatively, use John Innes No. 1 potting compost for young plants and No. 2 or No. 3 for established plants.

Repotting should be done when the compost in the pot is just moist.

To dislodge a pot-bound plant, place one hand over the compost, with the fingers either side of the plant stem. Invert the pot with the other hand and tap it firmly on the base to shake out the soil ball. If necessary, tap the pot against the edge of a table.

If there is a mass of intermingled roots with the soil ball, the plant needs moving into a larger-size pot. If not, return the plant to its pot with fresh compost.

With established plants, reduce the size of the soil ball by carefully easing the soil away and pulling away some of the roots.

If the pot is a clay one with a large drainage hole, place a crock – that is a piece of broken clay pot – over the hole, curved side up, to stop the compost falling through. Alternatively, use perforated zinc discs.

Plastic pots have several small drainage holes in their base and do not need any crocking.

Both types of pot should be scrubbed in water, especially on the inside, to eliminate disease organisms. New clay pots should be soaked in water for at least 12 hours, or they will draw moisture out of the compost.

Depending on the depth of the root ball, put a 1–2 in. layer of compost over the base of the pot.

Set the root ball on the compost so that the top is about ½ in. below the bottom of the rim of the pot.

Hold the plant steady in the centre with one hand, and with the fingers of the other hand trickle more compost into the space between root ball and pot. Cover the top of the ball with compost until it reaches the lower rim, then lightly thump the pot down on the working surface to settle the compost.

Top up with more compost to leave at least ½ in. space between compost and the top of the pot. Water in thoroughly, and firm lightly with the fingertips.

1 *Invert a pot-bound plant and shake out the soil-and-root ball*

2 *Before putting the plant in a larger pot, ease away some of the old soil*

3 *Set the root ball on fresh compost and trickle more compost around it*

4 *Water the plant thoroughly and firm the compost lightly with the fingers*

Keeping leaves shiny and dustfree

Plants breathe and absorb moisture from the air through their leaves. Both sides of the leaves should be kept clean to prevent clogging of the pores. Give small-leaved plants fine overhead sprays of clean water once a month, particularly during the growing season and if the plants are kept in coal-fired rooms.

Wipe both sides of large-leaved plants with a damp pad of cotton-wool from time to time. Dust-repelling liquids are available which impart a glossy sheen to the leaves at the same time as cleaning them.

Soft rain water is better than tap water both for watering and for cleaning. Set the house plants out-doors during soft warm rain showers, but bring them indoors again before nightfall.

Plants with soft hairy leaves, such as saintpaulia, must not be cleaned with water or proprietary leaf cleaners, as the leaves will become spotted. Use a fine paintbrush to remove any dust.

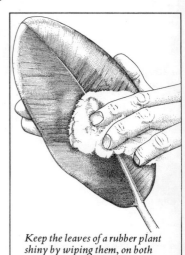
Keep the leaves of a rubber plant shiny by wiping them, on both sides, with damp cottonwool

Watering and feeding correctly

More house plants are killed by over-watering than by any other factor. The amount of water to be given depends on the type of plant, the room temperature and the time of year. Generally, house plants need more water during the growing or flowering season – late spring and summer – than during the resting period – autumn and winter. Narrow-leaved plants need more water than broad-leaved plants.

A copious watering once a week is better than a few drops every day. Tap water is normally quite satisfactory. But azaleas may develop yellow leaves if they are permanently watered with hard tap water, so use rain water whenever possible.

Long-stemmed and woody plants may be watered from the top of the pot, but tap water will eventually leave a lime deposit on the compost.

Rosette-type plants whose leaves grow straight from a low rootstock or corm, for example saintpaulia and cyclamen, should preferably not be watered from the top as this may cause rotting of the roots. Pour the water into the plant tray or saucer on which the pot stands and allow the compost to draw it up.

A badly dried-up plant can sometimes be revived by giving it a bath to ensure the root ball becomes thoroughly moist. Set the plant in a deep container and fill with water until this reaches the compost. As soon as air bubbles stop rising, the plant has had enough water.

Always avoid drops of water on hairy-leaved plants, such as gloxinia and saintpaulia. They cause discoloration and rotting of the leaves.

Liquid feed should be given during the growing season after the plants have been watered. Dissolve the feed in water according to the manufacturer's instructions, and water this on to the moist compost. One pint is generally sufficient to feed a dozen plants at a time.

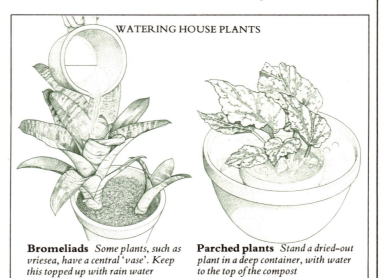

WATERING HOUSE PLANTS

Bromeliads *Some plants, such as vriesea, have a central 'vase'. Keep this topped up with rain water*

Parched plants *Stand a dried-out plant in a deep container, with water to the top of the compost*

Creating a humid atmosphere

Many house plants originated in tropical jungles and rain forests, where the atmosphere is always moist. Although they have in most cases adapted themselves to drier climates, they grow better when artificial humidity is provided, even during the dormant winter season.

Central heating creates a dry atmosphere in the house. To overcome the problem, provide humidity by placing shallow trays of water beside your house plants. Alternatively, set plant pots in a larger pot or decorative container and fill the space between them with peat kept moist all the time. This does not preclude regular watering of the plants themselves. Single pots can also be stood on trays or saucers of gravel. Pour water over the gravel as required, but do not let the water reach the base of the pots or rotting of the roots may occur. Spraying with water also improves humidity as well as keeping the leaves clean. On hot summer days a daily spraying is advisable.

Some plants, particularly those with hairy or soft leaves, benefit from an occasional steam treatment. Stand the pot in a large bowl supported on a bad heat conductor, such as a brick or a pudding basin, so that the leaves are kept clear of the bowl. Pour boiling water into the bowl and leave the plant until the water no longer gives off steam. A well-lit, warm bathroom is the ideal place for growing saintpaulias and other hairy-leaved plants.

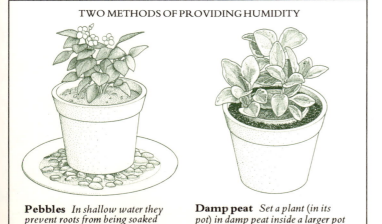

TWO METHODS OF PROVIDING HUMIDITY

Pebbles *In shallow water they prevent roots from being soaked*

Damp peat *Set a plant (in its pot) in damp peat inside a larger pot*

Steam treatment for hairy-leaved plants

Cutting back overgrown plants and training climbers

House plants need little or no pruning, but if they are growing straggly, shoots may be cut off cleanly just above a leaf joint.

Rubber plants and monstera that have grown too tall cannot be cut back without encouraging unwanted side-shoots. However, they can be restarted by cutting off the top shoot, about 12 in. long, below a node and inserting it in a pot of cuttings compost (p. 11).

To encourage the bushy or trailing habit of plants, pinch out the tips of young shoots in spring just above a leaf joint. This will produce side-shoots from the leaf axils.

Bushy and single-stemmed plants need no support, but climbing plants – such as the ivies and philodendrons – should be trained as soon as they are growing strongly. Insert bamboo canes in the pot and tie the shoots loosely into place with soft raffia or plastic rings, obtainable from florists' shops.

Triangular, square and circular trellis frames made of bamboo or plastic are also available.

Philodendrons and some other climbers develop aerial roots through which the plants obtain part of their nourishment. Such climbers are best trained on moss

TRAINING HOUSE PLANTS

Trailing plants *Pinch out tips to encourage side-shoots*

Climbers *Twine new shoots of ivy through trellis frames*

Aerial roots *Moss sticks are ideal for plants with aerial roots*

sticks – poles or circular frames filled with moss or other fibrous material. The moss must be kept constantly moist.

Looking after house plants during summer holidays

Before you go on holiday, arrange with a friend to look after your plants. If this is not possible, a few simple precautions will ensure that the plants will remain healthy for two or three weeks.

Remove all flowers and flower buds, pinching them off cleanly with the fingernails. This reduces the amount of water the plants will need.

Move the plants away from south or west-facing windows, out of direct sunlight.

Water the plants well, then pack them in deep boxes, surrounding them with wet, screwed-up newspaper or thoroughly soaked peat. Or, alternatively, water each plant thoroughly and cover with a polythene bag. Blow into the bag to extend it and keep it away from the leaves. Seal the bag around the pot with a rubber band.

Several automatic watering systems are available. However, the simplest watering for a number of plants is a home-made capillary system, using 1 in. lamp wicks.

Set a bucket of water on a brick or box on the draining board, or on a kitchen table. Arrange as many plants as possible round the bucket. Tie a small stone to one end of a lamp wick, and drop it into the

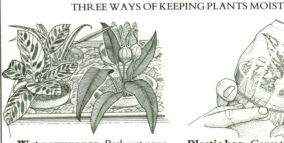

THREE WAYS OF KEEPING PLANTS MOIST

Wet newspaper *Pack wet newspaper or peat round pots in a box*

Plastic bag *Cover the plant with a plastic bag held by a rubber band*

Lamp wicks *Push a 1 in. lamp wick into the compost, with the other end in a bucket of water. This method lasts several weeks*

bucket. Insert the other end of the wick in the soil of a pot. (One wick for each plant.) The water will seep through the wicks and into the pots.

What can go wrong with house plants

Symptoms	Cause	Cure
Poor or absent blooms, weak and elongated stems, leaves smaller and paler than usual	Light deficiency	Increase existing light – if necessary with warm-white fluorescent tubes for flowering plants, and daylight fluorescent tubes for foliage plants
Lopside growth, with stems and leaves bending to one side	Light deficiency	Give the pot a quarter turn every other day to provide even light
Pale or brownish mottling, particularly on young leaves	Red spider mites, thrips	Spray with malathion
Plants stunted and with poor roots, often rotting or browning	Usually over-watering	Let plants dry out completely between waterings
Slow stem and leaf growth even when fed; soil dries out quickly, even after frequent watering; roots growing through drainage holes in pot	Pot-bound	Move plants into larger pots
Plants growing slowly or not at all	Under-feeding, over-watering or pot-bound	Feed regularly, reduce watering or pot on
Wilting	Soil or atmosphere too dry, too much sun or heat, over-watering, pot-bound	Spray leaves frequently, reduce watering and check on drainage, or move into larger pots
Sudden drop of buds, flowers and leaves	Usually a shock to the plant's system caused by a sudden change in temperature, light, increase of coal-gas fumes, prolonged cold draught or dryness of roots	Improve cultural conditions
Variegated leaves revert to green	Light deficiency or over-feeding	Cut off green leaves and move plant to a lighter position; reduce feeding
Brown edges or spots on leaves	Hot dry air, draughts, paraffin, coal-gas fumes, over-watering, sun-scorch, water splashes, over-feeding, pot-bound	Improve cultural conditions, pick off badly affected leaves
Yellow leaves which stay firm and healthy	Lime in compost, or tap water used for lime-hating plants	Repot in John Innes acid potting compost or a loamless compost, and water with rain water

Growing plants from fruit stones

Exotic and unusual additions to house-plant collections can be grown from the stones of many fruits, such as avocado pears, peaches and dates.

Peach and date stones can be put in 2–3 in. pots of seed compost, covered with black polythene and left to germinate at a temperature of 18°C (64°F). Peach stones should first be subjected to a temperature of 4°C (39°F) for several weeks before being planted.

To grow an avocado plant, insert three matchsticks to half their length into the soft stone. The object of bruising the stone is to stimulate rooting. Germination from stones is quickest in late summer.

Suspend the stone over the mouth of a jar of water. The water should reach to about ¾ in. below the base of the stone.

After six to eight weeks, thick white roots will appear. Pot the stone in a large pot of John Innes No. 1 compost and keep it in a well-lit, warm and humid place. Eventually, a single shoot will come up through the compost.

Avocado plants grow rapidly and need repotting annually; pinch out the growing shoot when the required height is reached.

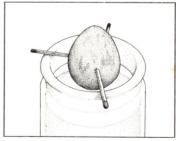

1 *Pierce the stone with matchsticks and suspend it over a jar of water*

Avocado plant grown from a stone

2 *After six to eight weeks, a number of brittle roots appear from the base*

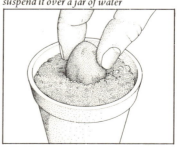

3 *Pot the stone, roots down, 2–3 in. deep in moist compost*

House plants/7

House plants from
pips of citrus fruit

Growing a
pineapple plant from
a fresh leafy top

House plants from pips of citrus fruit

Attractive, non-flowering plants can be grown from the pips of grapefruit, lemons and oranges. Plant the pips as soon as they are removed from the fruit.

Fill a 4 in. pot to within ½ in. of the top with a proprietary seed compost, or a compost made of 1 part loam and 1 part peat.

Water the compost thoroughly and bury the pips, four to six to each pot, ½ in. deep. Cover the pot loosely with a small sheet of polythene and secure with adhesive tape or a rubber band.

Germinate the pips at a temperature of 18°C (64°F); rooting should occur within a few weeks, and leaf-bearing shoots will appear through the compost.

Remove the polythene and leave the pot at the same temperature. When the plantlets are well established, plant them singly in 3–4 in. pots of John Innes No. 1 compost. They will eventually grow into 3–4 ft short-stemmed, bushy plants.

Pip-grown lemon tree

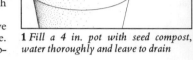

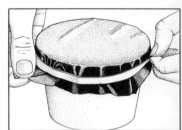

1 *Fill a 4 in. pot with seed compost, water thoroughly and leave to drain*

2 *Bury four to six fresh fruit pips and top with ½ in. of compost*

3 *Cover the pot loosely with a piece of polythene and secure with tape*

Growing a pineapple plant from a fresh leafy top

Slice the green, leafy top from a fresh pineapple, together with a narrow piece of flesh containing the top row of 'pips' on the skin. Dry off the top for one or two days.

Fill a 3½–4 in. pot to within ¾ in. of its top with moist potting compost; sprinkle a thin layer of coarse sand on top. Set the pineapple crown on the sand, and sprinkle a little more compost over the fleshy part.

Cover the pot with a polythene bag and put in a shaded position, at a temperature of 18°C (64°F). Rooting generally takes place in about eight weeks, and is indicated by the fresh appearance of the leaf tuft and possibly by new leaves.

Once growth is well established, remove the polythene and repot the plant in a larger pot.

The plant may grow to 2 ft high, but is unlikely to fruit unless given considerable humidity and warmth.

Young pineapple plant

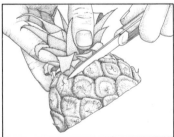

1 *Cut the crown and the top row of 'pips' from a fresh pineapple*

3 *Sprinkle fresh compost over the pineapple and firm with the fingers*

2 *Set the top on a shallow layer of coarse sand sprinkled over compost*

4 *Pull a clear polythene bag over the pot and secure with an elastic band*

Growing an indoor garden in a bottle

Bottles for indoor gardening are a 20th-century revival of the Victorian Wardian glass cases used for growing indoor ferns. Large carboys (acid bottles) make the most suitable containers, but any deep glass receptacle – fish bowls, confectionery jars, etc. – can be used, provided they have a large enough opening and can be kept airtight. The corked bottle acts as a miniature greenhouse. The continuous moisture given off from the plants and the compost, together with the light and the carbon dioxide exhaled by the plants, keep the trapped air pure.

Aeration of the soil in a closed bottle garden is extremely important, and the compost should therefore be more open and gritty than that used for pot plants. A peat-based compost mixed with a handful of crushed charcoal lumps is the ideal growing medium, as the charcoal helps to keep the compost aerated and sweet. Alternatively, use 2 parts of John Innes No. 1 potting compost to 1 part peat, and mix with a little crushed charcoal.

Clean and dry out the bottle thoroughly and put a 1 in. layer of gravel in the bottom if John Innes potting compost is used.

The compost should be dry, to prevent it sticking to the sides of the bottle; pour it into the bottle through a paper funnel, and let it settle to a depth of 3–4 in.

Moisten the compost evenly, using a small funnel fitted with a narrow plastic or rubber tube long enough to reach the compost.

Firm the compost with a cotton-reel wedged on the end of a stick before setting the plants in position.

Use a fork or dessertspoon, tied to a stick, to make shallow planting holes, starting at the outer edge of the compost.

Grip each plant with long-handled bamboo tweezers, or bend a piece of wire to fit the root ball.

Insert the plants into the holes, working from the outside inwards.

Firm the compost before positioning the next plant.

When all the plants have been sited, the bottle can be corked. The garden may then be left unattended for several months at a time. Remove the cork occasionally – every four months or so – to refresh the air. If necessary, give the plants a little liquid feed and water, using a funnel and narrow tube to prevent splashing the leaves and the bottle. If the bottle is left open, water it once a month.

Stand the bottle in a well-lit position, but out of direct sunlight, and turn it daily to give even light.

Only moisture-loving and slow-growing foliage plants should be used. Some ferns and bromeliads are suitable, but they will eventually outgrow their space.

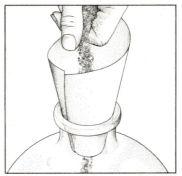

1 Insert a funnel in the bottle opening and trickle the compost through it

2 Use a fork, tied to a stick, to make planting holes in the moist compost

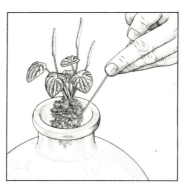

3 Loop a hooked wire round the roots and lower the plant into the bottle

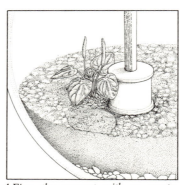

4 Firm the compost with an empty cotton-reel wedged on a stick

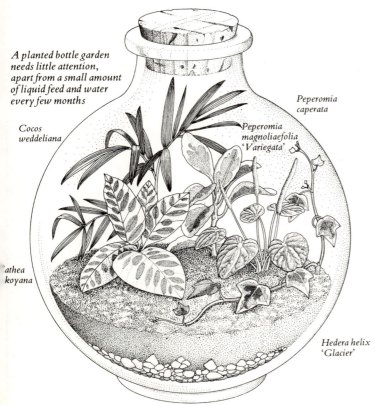

A planted bottle garden needs little attention, apart from a small amount of liquid feed and water every few months

Cocos
weddeliana

athea
koyana

Peperomia
magnoliaefolia
'Variegata'

Peperomia
caperata

Hedera helix
'Glacier'

House plants/9

How to grow new
house plants from old

*Dividing
multi-stemmed
house plants*

How to grow new house plants from old

Most house plants can be increased, some by simply dividing the plant into two or more pieces or by taking quick-rooting tip cuttings, and others by more complicated methods requiring artificial heat and moisture.

The following are the main propagation methods: division, air layering, cuttings of tip or side-shoots, leaf cuttings, offsets and plantlets.

Many house plants can also be raised from seeds. Most seedsmen and nurseries stock seeds of popular plants, such as begonias and impatiens, and some have seeds of more exotic plants, such as dizygotheca and fatsia. Most seeds germinate easily, but the plants will take a couple of years to reach maturity and need close attention and care during the early stages.

Sow the seeds during late spring or summer, in pots of seed compost.

Cover the seeds with a thin layer of sand or compost, and leave them to germinate, preferably at a temperature of 16–18°C (61–64°F).

As soon as the seedlings have developed two pairs of leaves, pot them singly into 2½–3 in. pots of John Innes No. 1 compost.

Keep the young plants well watered in a shaded, draught-proof place until new growth is evident. Gradually move the plants into more light, but away from draughts. Provide extra humidity and, when the plants are growing strongly, move them to their permanent positions.

Dividing multi-stemmed house plants

Division or splitting of a plant is the easiest method of propagation.

Only certain types of plants, however, can be increased in this way. Each plant must have at least two, and preferably several, stems arising from or below ground level, each stem with an independent, well-developed root system.

Suitable plants include adiantum (maidenhair fern), asparagus (asparagus fern), chlorophytum (spider plant), aspidistra, fittonia and sansevieria (mother-in-law's tongue).

House plants can be divided at any time during the growing period, from late spring to early autumn.

Knock the plant out of its pot, and tease away the soil round the crown and root ball, using a small stick or your fingers. This will expose the rootstock and the points at which the plant can be divided.

Grasp the base of the plant in both hands and pull it gently but firmly apart. If the crown or rootstock is thick and tough, sever the largest roots or the underground stems with a sharp knife.

Pot the separated pieces at once in John Innes No. 2 compost.

Water sparingly at first and keep the pots in a shaded warm position for a few weeks.

Certain house plants, especially beloperone, tradescantia, pilea and zebrina, are often grown commercially from three or more cuttings in the same small pot. As the cuttings grow, they form one single plant which can later be divided by pulling it carefully apart. Pot up the separate pieces.

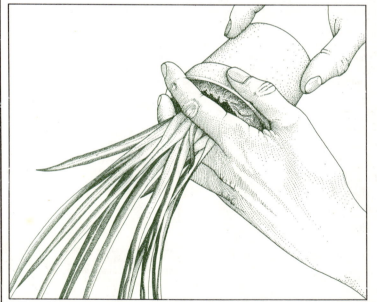

1 *Invert the pot and place your fingers around the stems; knock the rim of the pot against the edge of a table to dislodge the compost and the roots*

2 *Ease away the compost and carefully pull the roots of the plant apart*

3 *Cut any intertangled roots free with a sharp knife or a razor blade*

4 *Set each division in a pot of John Innes No. 2 potting compost*

5 *Fill up with more compost, and level it ½ in. below the top of the pot*

Taking tip cuttings from non-flowering stems

Cuttings from hollow-stemmed plants, such as impatiens and tradescantia, and from ivy root extremely easily.

Take cuttings from the tips of young, non-flowering stems or sideshoots, between June and August. Strip the lower leaves from a 3–4 in. cutting, and trim it cleanly just below a leaf node. Stand the cutting in a glass of tap water; roots will appear within 10–14 days and the cutting can then be potted up.

With other house plants, insert the cuttings at once in a rooting medium.

Fill a 3½ in. pot to just below the rim with a mixture of equal quantities of peat and coarse sand, or a proprietary cuttings compost.

Using a sharp knife, cut off the top 3–4 in. of a stem or side-shoot. Pull off the lower leaves and make a clean cut across the stem, just below a leaf node.

With a small dibber or stick make a number of 1–1½ in. deep planting holes in the compost – a 3½ in. pot will accommodate four to six cuttings. Make the holes round the edge of the pot so that the stems are supported on the rim.

Firm the compost gently round each cutting. Fill the pot to the rim with water and leave to drain.

Cover the pot loosely with a polythene bag and secure with a rubber band. Set the pot in a shaded position where a temperature of 18°C (64°F) can be maintained. Keep the compost moist.

After three or four weeks the cuttings should have rooted, and the tips will be showing fresh growth.

Remove the polythene bag, and carefully invert the pot. Separate the rooted cuttings carefully, and pot singly in 3–3½ in. pots of John Innes No. 1 compost.

Water carefully, and keep the plants in a shaded, draught-free place until they are growing well.

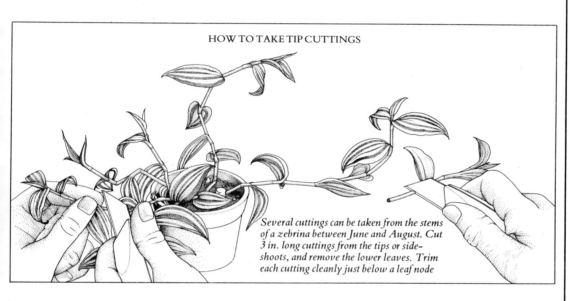

HOW TO TAKE TIP CUTTINGS

Several cuttings can be taken from the stems of a zebrina between June and August. Cut 3 in. long cuttings from the tips or side-shoots, and remove the lower leaves. Trim each cutting cleanly just below a leaf node

ROOTING TIP CUTTINGS

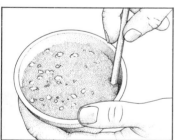

1 *Make four to six planting holes round the edge of a 3½ in. pot*

2 *Insert each cutting so that the stem rests against the pot*

3 *Cover with polythene, and keep in shade until the cuttings are rooted*

4 *Tip up the pot, and carefully separate the rooted cuttings*

5 *Pot the new plants singly in 3–3½ in. pots of John Innes No. 1 compost*

6 *Water the potted cuttings and keep in a shaded place for a few weeks*

Removing rooted offsets from suckering plants

Most of the bromeliads, such as billbergia, aechmea and vriesea, as well as other house plants (fatsia, hippeastrum and aglaonema) readily produce offsets or suckers. These small plants, which appear at the base of the parent, may eventually overcrowd the pot.

Offsets which have reached about half the height of the parent plant can be easily removed and potted up separately. The best time for this type of propagation is between June and August.

Knock the plant from its pot, placing the fingers of one hand round the stems and inverting the pot with the other hand. If necessary, tap the pot against the workbench to loosen the root ball.

Remove the plant from the pot and crumble away the soil.

Hold the root ball, stems up, in one hand and tear or cut away the offset complete with roots, but take care not to break them.

Put a layer of moist John Innes No. 2 compost in a 3–4 in. pot, and set the offset on top so that the top of the crown is ½ in. below the rim of the pot. Trickle in more compost and firm with the fingertips. Fill the pot with water and allow to drain.

Tall offsets will need staking for one or two months, until the root systems are well established. Insert a bamboo cane close to the plant and secure with one or two ties.

Set the plant in a well-lit position, but out of direct sunlight for a couple of weeks. A north-west-facing window-sill is the ideal place. Keep the compost moist.

1 *Knock pot of congested billbergia firmly to loosen the root ball*

2 *Pull the rooted offset away without damaging the roots*

3 *Insert the offset in a 3–4 in. pot of compost; firm with the fingers*

4 *Tie tall offsets to bamboo stakes for a few weeks; keep moist*

Detaching and rooting plants from runners

Some plants, notably saxifraga and chlorophytum, produce small plants either on the flowering spikes or on thin runners from the parent plant.

On saxifraga detach the thread-like runners, each of which bears a plantlet, from the parent plant. Nip off the runner from the plantlet.

Fill a 2½ in. pot with moist John Innes No. 1 compost to within ½ in. of the rim.

Make a shallow depression in the surface and set the plantlet in it. Firm the compost round the base of the plant.

Do not water, but place a polythene bag over the pot and secure with a rubber band.

Keep the pot out of direct sunlight and at a temperature of 18–21°C (64–70°F). Check that the compost remains moist.

After about ten days, the plantlet should have rooted. Remove the bag and set the pot in a lighter and cooler place.

Chlorophytum often bears a number of plantlets on tough stalks. These can be layered into individual 2 in. pots of John Innes No. 2 compost and secured with wire staples. After about three weeks, the plantlets should have rooted and the stalks can be severed.

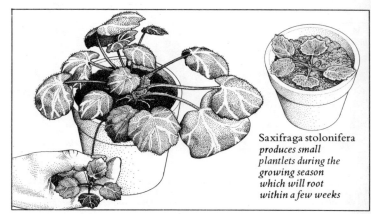

Saxifraga stolonifera *produces small plantlets during the growing season which will root within a few weeks*

Leaf cuttings from hairy or fleshy-leaved plants

House plants with thick, hairy or fleshy leaves, such as saintpaulia, begonia, sinningia (gloxinia) and peperomia, are increased by leaf cuttings.

The best time for this propagation method is from June to September.

To grow new plants from old, cut two or three healthy leaves, each with a 1–1½ in. stalk, from the plant.

Almost fill a 3½ in. pot with a mixture of equal quantities of peat and coarse sand, or a proprietary cuttings compost. Make two or three planting holes, slightly less deep than the stalks.

Trim the end of each leaf stalk

cleanly across with a sharp knife.

Insert the leaf stalks into the holes. The base of each stalk should just touch the bottom of the hole, but the leaf itself must be clear of the compost, or rotting may occur.

Firm the cuttings gently with the fingertips, taking care not to bruise the slender stalks.

Ideally, the cuttings should be left to root in a propagating unit with additional heat, but a close and warm atmosphere can easily be provided in the home. Fill the pot to the top with water and let it drain thoroughly, then enclose it in a polythene bag. Secure the bag with

a rubber band, and take care not to let the compost dry out. A moist compost, however, may cause condensation on the inside of the bag. If this happens, remove the bag and turn it inside out before replacing it.

After three to five weeks, roots should have formed, and new leaves will appear from the base of the leaf stem. Invert the pot and separate the rooted cuttings carefully, without breaking the fine roots. Pot the cuttings singly in 2½ in. pots of John Innes No. 1 compost. Water and drain thoroughly. Keep the plants in a shaded, warm position for two or three weeks.

Leaf cuttings from hairy or fleshy-leaved plants

HOW TO TAKE LEAF CUTTINGS

Between June and September, cut young healthy leaves, with stalks attached, from a saintpaulia (African violet). Trim the stalks cleanly

ROOTING LEAF CUTTINGS FROM SAINTPAULIAS

1 *With a small stick make a few planting holes in a pot of compost*

2 *Insert each cutting so that the leaf blade is just above the compost*

3 *Firm the compost with the fingers, avoiding damaging the stalks*

4 *Fill the pot with water to the top and let it drain completely*

5 *Cover the pot with a polythene bag, secured with a rubber band*

6 *When new leaves have grown, pot each cutting in potting compost*

Raising several new plants from one leaf

Several new plants can be grown from one leaf, if it is large enough, as in the case of *Begonia rex*.

At any time between June and September, detach a mature leaf and trim the stalk to within ½–1 in. of the leaf base. Using a sharp knife, make a number of cuts on the underside where the main veins join.

Place the leaf, cut side down, on a seed pan of moist John Innes No. 1 potting compost. Secure the leaf with pebbles or crocks. Cover the pan with polythene and place it in a temperature of 21°C (70°F), plantlets will appear from the cuts.

Remove the polythene, and leave the pan in a warm, shady place for another two or three weeks.

Pot the rooted plantlets individually in 2½ in. pots of potting compost.

1 *Increase* Begonia rex *and other begonias from leaf cuttings*

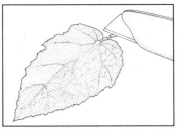

2 *Select a leaf and trim the stalk to about ½ in. from the leaf base*

4 *Lay the leaf, cut side down, on the compost and weight it down with crocks*

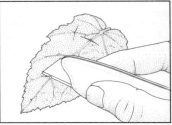

3 *Make cuts on the underside of the leaf where the main veins meet*

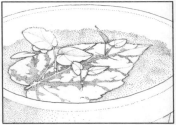

5 *After a few weeks, plantlets will appear from the cut intersections*

Increasing sansevieria from leaf sections

The leaves of sansevieria can be cut into horizontal sections, each of which will produce a new plant.

During spring or summer, select a one-year-old healthy leaf and cut it away close to the crown.

Fill a 5 in. pot with moist John Innes No. 1 compost.

Using a sharp knife, cut the leaf crossways into 1 in. deep sections.

Insert three or four sections, lower side down, in the compost to half their depth. Spray with tepid water, and place a polythene bag over the pot. Keep in a shaded position at a temperature of 21°C (70°F).

When each section begins to produce a leaf, after about six weeks, remove the polythene and pot the young plants singly in 3 in. pots of John Innes No. 1 compost.

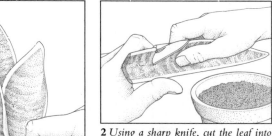

1 *Cut a sansevieria leaf away from the crown of the parent plant*

2 *Using a sharp knife, cut the leaf into 1 in. deep horizontal sections*

3 *Insert the sections, lower side down, in a pan of moist potting compost*

4 *Cover with a polythene bag to create a humid atmosphere*

5 *After six weeks the leaf sections will develop into young plants*

Propagating plants by air layering

After some years dizygothecas and rubber plants (ficus) may grow too tall, and will often lose their lower leaves. Rather than throw the plant out, propagate it by the air-layering method in spring to produce a new, shorter-stemmed plant.

Using a sharp knife, remove the leaves 6–9 in. below the growing tip. Cut them flush with the stem, without damaging the tissues.

Then make an upward-slanting cut about 1½ in. long, starting below a leaf node. Tie the stem to a stake above and below the cut.

Prop the cut open with a matchstick, and brush both sides with hormone rooting powder.

Remove the stick and fold clear polythene around the cut. The polythene should be about 6–7 in. wide and long enough to come 3–4 in. below and above the cut. Seal with adhesive tape below the cut, to create a tube or sleeve.

Fill the tube with thoroughly moistened sphagnum moss or peat, pressing it into and around the cut with a small stick. Seal the top of the tube with tape, so that the rooting medium will remain moist.

After eight to ten weeks the cut should have produced roots.

Sever the shoot below the tube and carefully free the roots from the polythene and moss. Discard the old plant or let it grow on to produce side-shoots.

Pot the new plant in a 4 in. pot of John Innes No. 2 compost. For the first two or three weeks, until the new root system is established, grow the plant in a temperature of 18–21°C (64–70°F) and syringe the leaves daily with water.

Propagating plants by air layering

1 *In spring, remove any leaves about 6–9 in. below the top cluster on an overgrown rubber plant. Cut the leaves flush with the stem*

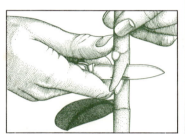

2 *Make a slanting, upward cut, 1½–2 in. long, from below a leaf node*

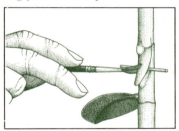

3 *Open out the cut carefully and brush with hormone rooting powder*

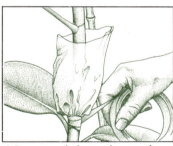

4 *Secure a polythene tube over the cut with adhesive tape*

5 *Pack the polythene with moist sphagnum moss and seal the tube*

6 *When roots become visible, sever the shoot just below them*

7 *Pot the new rubber plant in John Innes No. 2 potting compost*

Cacti/1

Introduction

With their bizarre shapes, varied textures and often vivid blossoms, cacti and other succulents are among the most intriguing of house and greenhouse plants

Plants that store water in their tissues during rainy seasons, and draw on it in periods of drought, are called succulents. There are two main types: those that store the water in their leaves and those that store it in their stems.

Cacti, the largest single family of succulents, are the best known examples of the stem type, and the various shapes into which their stems have developed hold a great fascination for gardeners.

Many people who do not have a garden find this no bar to collecting cacti as a hobby for, although a greenhouse is ideal, there are plenty of varieties that will flourish in a warm conservatory or on sunny window-sills, where their bizarre shapes give an original touch to any indoor display of pot plants.

Some of the most spectacular types which might have impressed travellers abroad need the long, hot summers that are rare in the British Isles. But there are many other cacti which will do well in our cooler climate.

It is not always easy to differentiate cacti from other stem succulents – they are sometimes very similar in form. The one reliable distinguishing feature is the areoles that cacti always bear. These are small, cushion-like structures on the stems, from which spines and flowers are produced.

Cacti are thought of as plants from parched areas, but they rarely grow in areas where the rainfall is less than 10 in. a year – although some have survived in areas where only 3–4 in. has been recorded.

Cacti also need mineral salts to survive, and although deserts are normally considered to be barren land, the soil is in fact often rich in minerals that originate in weathered rocks.

Desert cacti often receive their year's supply of water in the course of a very short rainy season, during which they grow and flower. Many need a cool, dry winter rest period. The reason that few can survive outdoors in a British winter is not just the cold, but the combination of cold and wet soil conditions.

The desert cacti vary greatly in form. They may grow as columns over 40 ft high, or as tiny spheres less than 1 in. in diameter. Their stems are usually covered in either wax or hairs, which reduce water loss from evaporation.

The stems of some other succulents are 'mealy' – covered with a substance which looks like small, powdery porridge oats. This is another method by which cacti reduce water evaporation.

Cacti are usually green, as they contain chlorophyll and carry out photosynthesis, a process normally performed by leaves. Their root systems are extensive, some near the surface to catch dew, others deep delving to pick up ground water low down.

Many desert cacti have spines, which act as a defence against animals trying to eat them.

Cacti also occur in wet forests in Central and South America, where they grow with their roots in the debris that collects in the crotches of trees. Usually these cacti, which include the popular Christmas cactus and the Easter cactus, have flattened, leaf-like stems.

Contrary to the popular belief that they flower only every seven years, most cacti bloom regularly, if they are given the right conditions – although the very large cacti will not flower in a greenhouse that does not allow them to achieve their full size.

The typical flowers are trumpet-shaped, and they vary in size from $\frac{3}{8}$ in. to 6 in. across. Usually they open only in warm sunshine, but there are some whose flowers are seen only at night. If there is prolonged cloud, the flower buds may not develop at all.

In general, cactus flowers are more showy than those of other succulents. The blooms come in many colours, except pure blue, though there are many shades of mauve and violet. Most nocturnal-flowering types are white, and often carry a sweet, lily-like scent. This attracts night-flying moths, which pollinate the flowers. Most cactus flowers last only for a day or two.

Seed pods sometimes appear if the flowers have been pollinated successfully. They are often brightly coloured, as in the case of the mammillarias, many of which will produce them without artificial pollination methods being employed. The pods are mostly various shades of red and are long-lasting.

Seed pods may take a long time to form. A whole year may elapse after pollination has taken place, so that one year's flowers and the previous year's pods sometimes appear on the same cactus.

Nearly all 1700 species of cactus are native to Mexico, western and southern USA and South America.

Some succulents that are not true cacti, however, are native to Britain. These are the stonecrops, or sedums, that grow on rocks, walls, steep banks or cliffs, where the soil may be very shallow and soon dries, even though heavy rain may have fallen.

Species that can be found in this country are *Sedum acre*, *S. album*, *S. anglicum*, *S. reflexum*, *S. roseum* and *S. telephium*.

The pennywort, *Umbilicus rupestris*, is fairly common in the western parts of the British Isles and is easily recognised by its round, dimpled, shiny leaves about the size of an old penny piece and, in summer, its drooping green-white flowers, carried on a stem up to 15 in. long.

Native British succulents *The most common succulents native to the British Isles are the stonecrops, or sedums (left), found on rocks, banks and cliffs. The pennywort (right) is also fairly common in western parts of the British Isles, where it grows in stony places, particularly drystone walls*

The care of cacti in the house

Nearly all cacti originated in deserts, and so enjoy bright sunlight.

To grow the widest range, a heated greenhouse with a minimum winter temperature of 5°C (41°F) is necessary. But many cacti can be grown as house plants in a south or west-facing window, provided they are put outdoors in a sunny place during the summer.

A few cacti originated in tropical rain forests and require shady growing conditions. If plants are to be kept indoors permanently, these forest cacti, such as epiphyllums, rhipsalidopsis and schlumbergeras, are good choices. Keep them in a position beside an east or north-facing window.

Mis-shapen growth *Lack of light has distorted this flat-stemmed opuntia. Rotate plants receiving light from a window, to ensure even growth*

It is better to use tap water than rain water when watering cacti. Rain water can contain bacteria and fungi that might harm the plants.

Central heating causes problems for desert cacti, which need a cold, dry winter rest in order to flower well. In winter they should be kept in an unheated room, where the temperature remains between 5°C (41°F) and 10°C (50°F). Otherwise the high temperature, and the need consequently for watering to prevent the plants from shrivelling, may cause them to grow in the wrong season. It is better to keep them in a dry cold frame in winter than in a centrally heated room.

Do not shut them between the curtains and the window on winter nights, as they may be damaged by a pocket of cold air.

What can go wrong with cacti

Apart from the troubles pinpointed in the table, cacti are susceptible to several common greenhouse pests, such as ants, scale insects, thrips and woodlice. Spray these pests with a systemic insecticide as soon as they appear.

Root mealy bugs, which cause discoloration, are less common, but discourage them by watering compost with a malathion solution.

Symptoms	Cause	Cure
Corky, pale brown patches	Old damage by mealy bugs or red spiders; erratic watering	No remedy, though healthy tops can be severed and rooted as cuttings
Distinct rings of growth, getting progressively smaller towards the top of the plant	Too little water plus starvation	Repot or feed during the growing season. Water correctly
Wrinkling and softening; little or no growth	Too little water; root rot	Water correctly
Fluffy patches of whitish, waxy wool	Mealy bugs	Spray with malathion or wipe over with methylated spirit
Thin, pale, sappy growth	Too shaded; too much heat at the wrong time of year (usually in winter)	Keep in a sunny site and follow a correct heating regime
Base becomes soft and wet, followed by the collapse of whole or part of plant	Basal stem rot	No cure, but firm, green tip may be severed and rooted
Yellowish or brownish mottling	Red spider mites	Spray with malathion, formothion, dimethoate or derris

Growing cacti out of doors

The tougher, larger cacti can be used to make an exotic display in the open garden, while they are getting their summer sun. But first take cuttings (see p. 20) to maintain your stock if they become too big to return indoors, or become straggly.

Add extra grit to a south-facing garden bed to ensure good drainage. Then put the plants into the bed.

The large opuntias make good background plants. *Opuntia robusta* and *O. tuna* become tree-like and grow 2–3 ft high. Avoid delicate species such as *O. microdasys*.

The columnar cereus also make good background plants.

Smaller plants, such as the 3–6 in. echeverias or sempervivums, can be planted between the larger plants.

Outdoor cactus gardens blend well with yuccas, herbaceous perennials that come from the same desert areas.

Cactus gardens should be regarded as summer gardens only, and the plants discarded or returned to the greenhouse in autumn. In mild areas they may overwinter successfully.

Succulents with a decorative covering of 'meal' on their leaves need to be given protection from the rain if put out of doors.

The sturdier cacti and other succulents can be planted out of doors in a well-drained site facing south, to provide an exotic summer display

When plants need repotting

Cacti need to be repotted when the mineral salts in their compost have been absorbed by the plant, or washed away by the water or, in the case of vigorous, young specimens, when the roots have filled the pot. Inspect the roots of new plants after you have bought them.

Ideally, repotting is carried out in the spring, but it can be done at any time of the year. It provides an opportunity to check the roots for pests, especially root mealy bugs.

Disinfect new pots to prevent them spreading pests or disease.

A moist, well-drained compost is essential. Use equal parts of John Innes No. 2 compost and a coarse sand, or a soil-less potting compost.

Tap the pot against a work bench to loosen the soil ball. If tapping fails, push a pencil through the central hole in the base of the pot.

Remove the plant, using a folded newspaper to protect your hands.

Take care to disturb the roots as little as possible. Old caked soil should be taken from the base of the plant and loose soil shaken off.

Take a pot one size larger than the old one and, if it is a clay pot, put a crock over the central hole.

Hold the plant in the centre of the pot and pour in new compost, ensuring it does not rise above the old soil mark on the stem. Spread the compost round the plant with a spoon.

Tap the pot on the working surface to settle the compost down.

Withhold water for a few days to prevent rotting of damaged roots.

Large plants seldom need repotting, but the top layer of compost should occasionally be renewed.

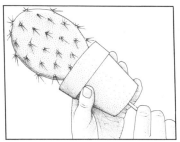

1 *A pencil through the central hole will loosen plants*

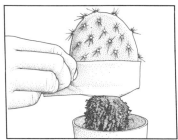

2 *Use a folded newspaper to protect your hands against spines*

3 *Remove old soil from the base of the plant and shake off loose soil*

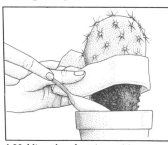

4 *Holding the plant in position, spread new compost round it with a spoon*

When to water and how to feed

Cacti should be watered in the growing period whenever the soil looks dry. When dormant they need no water at all, or just enough to prevent the soil drying out completely. However, if kept in a living-room, more water should be given. Exceptions are the forest cacti, such as epiphyllums; keep these damp in winter. Over-watering can rot the roots. Lithops (stone plants) need special watering (see below).

Every fortnight during the flowering period, give plants a liquid feed with tomato fertiliser, at the same strength as for tomatoes.

WATERING

Stand pots in water until the surface of the compost is damp

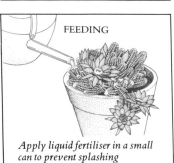

FEEDING

Apply liquid fertiliser in a small can to prevent splashing

WATERING STONE PLANTS

1 *Lithops and conophytums, the stone plants, should not be watered after late autumn*

2 *In spring the new plant emerges, but water only when the old leaves have become dry*

Cleaning cacti

To prevent plants with shiny stems or pads becoming dusty in the house, wipe them occasionally with a damp sponge. This helps them to breathe and absorb sunlight.

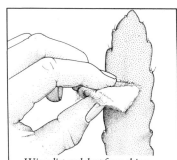

Wipe dirt and dust from shiny plants, especially in industrial areas

Growing new plants from cuttings

Taking cuttings is the simplest and most generally used method of propagating cacti and succulents.

A piece of the stem is cut off with a sharp knife or a razor blade and is rooted in compost.

If the plant is of a type that has individual leaves, a leaf can easily be removed and made to root.

Some plants produce offsets, or smaller versions of the parent plant, which need only to be cut away and potted in compost. Some of these offsets are already equipped with their own roots. No harm is done to the parent plant by taking cuttings, it will continue to grow normally.

Advice on how to propagate each type of plant is given in the following pages.

Apart from pereskia cuttings, which should be potted up as soon as they are taken, cuttings of cacti must be left to dry until the cut surface has formed a callus. The time taken ranges from one or two days for the small wound of opuntias, to five days or a week for the large-stemmed cerei.

The drying-off period is essential to avoid rotting – the main danger to these cuttings. For the same reason, cactus cuttings should not be covered with propagating covers or polythene to aid rooting.

May and June, the period of maximum growth, is the best time to take cuttings, but they can be taken at other times if necessary: for example, when plants drop their leaves or make leggy growth their tops can be removed and treated as cuttings.

The time taken for cuttings to root varies from one plant to another, but it is indicated by signs of new growth.

Cuttings should never be taken out of the compost before growth has appeared on them, as this disturbance can cause damage to the embryo roots of the young plant.

How to take stem cuttings of cacti

To take a stem cutting, remove a horizontal section of stem – whether globular, columnar, strap-like or segmented – by cutting the stem straight across.

Use a sharp knife or a razor blade, except for tough-stemmed plants such as epiphyllums which will require cutting with secateurs.

Slender-stemmed columnar cacti yield enough material for several cuttings from one stem. Make sure that you know which is the top and which the bottom of each section. Their growth will be distorted if they are put into the compost the wrong way up.

With opuntias, each cutting should normally be one complete segment or more, cut off at the joints. With small-jointed cacti, such as Christmas cactus, each cutting should consist of two or three segments. Put all cuttings in a warm, dry place for about three days, to allow a callus to form on the wound.

Once calluses have formed, fill a $2\frac{1}{2}$ in. pot to within $\frac{1}{2}$ in. of the top with moist, sandy compost, such as equal parts of John Innes No. 2 potting compost and coarse sand or grit. Insert the cuttings into the compost, just deep enough to keep them in an upright position.

Keep the compost just moist. Over-watering can rot cuttings.

Stem cuttings should root after one to three weeks. The time varies according to the genus.

They should then be potted individually into pots containing the same sort of compost as before. The pots should be large enough to hold the plant's root system comfortably.

1 Slice through the stem with secateurs or a sharp knife

2 Put cuttings in a warm, dry place until a callus forms

3 Insert cuttings into compost, just deep enough to keep them upright

4 When cuttings show signs of growth, remove and pot them on

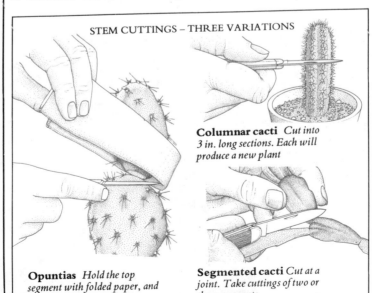

STEM CUTTINGS – THREE VARIATIONS

Opuntias *Hold the top segment with folded paper, and cut at the joint*

Columnar cacti *Cut into 3 in. long sections. Each will produce a new plant*

Segmented cacti *Cut at a joint. Take cuttings of two or three segments*

Taking cuttings from leafy plants

Many succulent plants, such as echeverias, sedums, crassulas and haworthias, can be reproduced from single leaves.

Pull the leaves from the plant with your fingers or tweezers and allow them to dry for a day or two.

Then insert them in a moist, sandy compost, just deep enough to ensure they stay upright. If inserted too deep, they will rot.

Small cylindrical or globular leaf cuttings may be simply laid flat on the surface, and if kept moist they will root.

Cuttings of both types will usually root in about a fortnight.

Rooting is then followed by the appearance of a small leaf cluster. This will grow rapidly to form a rosette of branching leaves.

At this stage, the cutting is potted on into a 2–2½ in. pot, containing equal parts of John Innes No. 2 compost and coarse sand.

The parent leaf should not be removed until it has withered.

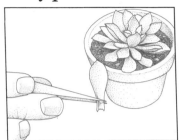

1 *Carefully remove a leaf from the plant with fingers or tweezers*

2 *Do not push in the leaf too deeply – just enough to hold it up*

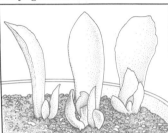

3 *The appearance of shoots beside the leaf shows the cutting has taken*

4 *When the rosette reaches leaf height, the cutting is ready for potting on*

Propagating from offsets, offshoots and by division

Some cacti and other succulents produce young plantlets which appear round the base and are miniature versions of the parent plants. These offsets usually come from below ground level, or from low lateral shoots on the plant.

Certain cacti, such as some echin-opsis and rebutia, produce offsets which have their own root systems. They can be detached and potted up as separate, young plants. These offsets should not be detached from the parent until the roots have developed.

Other offsets have no roots. They can be cut away, dried off, pressed slightly into moist, sandy compost and treated as cuttings.

Sometimes confused with offsets are offshoots – lateral branches sent out by the stumps of plants after cuttings have been taken from them. Offshoots can be treated as cuttings. While the stump continues to grow new offshoots it can be kept, but once it stops it should be discarded.

Division
Succulents that resemble clusters of stones can be divided.

Loosen the soil around the base of one of the plantlets and tear it away from its neighbour, making sure a small piece of stem comes with it.

If no tissue is torn, the plantlet can be potted immediately.

If tissue is torn, dry the plant off for a few days, and then insert it in compost in the normal way.

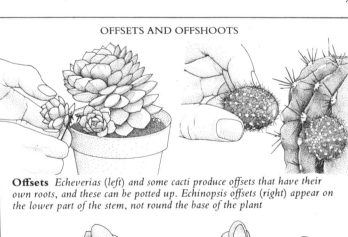

OFFSETS AND OFFSHOOTS

Offsets *Echeverias (left) and some cacti produce offsets that have their own roots, and these can be potted up. Echinopsis offsets (right) appear on the lower part of the stem, not round the base of the plant*

Offshoots *Growths from a stump from which cuttings have been taken are known as offshoots. They also make good cuttings*

Lithops and conophytums are propagated by pulling off one plantlet and potting it

Propagating cacti by grafting

Although it is possible to graft other succulent plants as well as cacti, this is difficult and not often undertaken. In any case, most succulents are propagated more easily by cuttings. All grafted succulents you are likely to see, therefore, are cacti.

Grafting consists of bringing together the upper part of one plant, called the scion, and the rootstock of another, called the stock, so that they form one plant.

It is usually carried out on plants which are difficult to grow on their own root systems, on plants that contain no chlorophyll and have been artificially kept alive, or on those that cannot easily be grown from seed, offsets or cuttings.

Usually there is no significant difference between grafted cacti and those grown naturally, especially if the rootstock is concealed. But sometimes the union of two species accelerates growth in a way that is not typical of the species.

Though many amateur growers shrink from grafting because it appears such drastic treatment, it is a fairly simple process. It is best done sometime between May and August, in a dry atmosphere with a temperature of 19–21°C (66–70°F). Any strong-growing cactus can be used as rootstock, but it must bear some relation to the size of the cactus to be grafted.

Usually, the aim is to make the graft as unobtrusive as possible, and this can be done by hiding the neck of the rootstock with pebbles.

But grafting can also be used to produce an unusual shape, as when a trailing cactus on a columnar one gives a 'weeping' plant.

WHY CACTI ARE GRAFTED

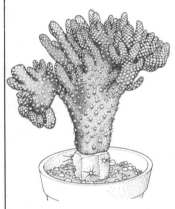

Weak roots *Some cacti such as* Opuntia claveroides *have weak roots and need a stronger rootstock*

Propagation *Cacti that do not easily grow from seed, cuttings or offsets are increased by grafting*

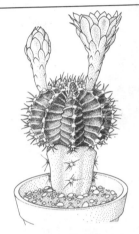

No chlorophyll *Coloured types such as the gymnocalycium 'Black Cap' need a green rootstock*

Cactus species suitable as rootstocks

Cacti which provide the rootstock for grafting should be easy to grow and propagate. The most usual stock for grafting is trichocereus, a columnar cactus which can be grown easily from seed. Most species of it are suitable, but species with smaller spines such as *Trichocereus spachianus* are easier to use.

One-year-old trichocereus seedlings can be used for grafting small scions. The cut tops can be rooted and grown on to take larger scions.

The softer-stemmed echinocereus species also make useful stock, especially for sickly, rather dried scions. Suitable species are *Echinocereus dubius, E. enneacanthus* and *E. pentalophus.* They branch freely and root easily, and so can be freely propagated by stem cuttings. Pads of *Opuntia robusta,* about 1–2 in. high, also make good rootstock.

Echinopsis species such as *Echinopsis eyriesii* and its hybrids are sometimes useful, as they form offsets prolifically. Mostly globular, they root easily and quickly, and can be used for grafting when about $\frac{3}{4}$–1 in. across. A section is cut from the top to correspond to the diameter of the scion, and the graft is made in the usual way.

How to graft a columnar cactus

A vigorous, well-rooted rootstock, about the same size as the plant to be grafted (the scion), is essential. Trichocereus is the most common rootstock.

Cut off the top of the rootstock with a sharp, clean razor blade. The top section can be dried and rooted for future use (see p. 20).

Chamfer the edges of the stock with a razor blade, to remove any spines and prevent the surface becoming concave.

Cut the plant to be grafted in a similar manner. Both surfaces to be joined must be level and smooth.

Press the scion on the freshly cut stock with a rotary motion, which will remove air bubbles. Try to match up the central bundle of tissues, which carries sap around the plant. This is in the form of a ring, which varies in diameter from 1 in. in the larger plants to $\frac{1}{4}$–$\frac{1}{2}$ in. in the smaller.

Place rubber bands round the top of the scion and the base of the pot. A piece of cottonwool can be placed on top of the scion to prevent the rubber bands bruising it.

The grafted plant should be placed in a warm, shady part of the greenhouse or house and watered.

After one or two weeks, the scion should be attached to the rootstock. The rubber bands can then be carefully removed.

If the graft has not taken, the two parts will separate at a touch.

If more than one offspring is required from the original scion, sever it once it shows signs of growth, leaving about ½ in. of scion on the rootstock.

Graft the severed portion on to another rootstock.

Offsets will form around the ½ in. of scion remaining on the first rootstock. When they are about ½ in. in diameter, remove them and root them, or re-graft.

1 *Slice off the top of the rootstock with a sharp knife or razor blade*

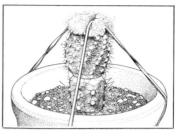

2 *Chamfer the edges with a razor blade, removing the spines*

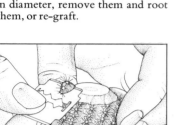

3 *Treat the scion in the same way, so that the edges match up*

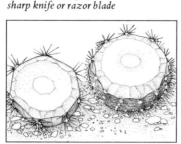

4 *Match up the central bundle of tissues, which carries food*

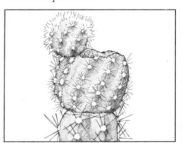

5 *Keep scion in place with rubber bands; cottonwool protects it*

6 *About two weeks later, carefully remove the rubber bands*

7 *To grow more plants, remove the top of the scion and graft it*

8 *Offsets on the portion of scion left can be treated as cuttings*

How to wedge graft a flat-stemmed cactus

Opuntia grafting

How to wedge graft a flat-stemmed cactus

Flat-stemmed plants such as Christmas and Easter cacti are grafted in a different way from columnar cacti, because of their shape. This method is known as a wedge graft.

A useful rootstock is a stout opuntia pad of the kind formed by *Opuntia robusta*.

Cut a slit in the top of the pad using a sharp, clean knife or a razor blade. Shape the base of the scion's pad into a wedge, and quickly insert it into the slot in the pad of the rootstock.

To hold the graft in position, pass an opuntia spine through it. Do not use a pin, as it will corrode. Keep the plant warm and watered in the normal way. Once the graft has taken, about four to six weeks later, the spine can be removed.

This type of grafting is used for much-branched, cascading plants that are difficult to manage.

Christmas cacti and Easter cacti are also sometimes grafted on to pereskia stems to give a 'standard' effect. Grow them at 10°C (50°F).

Opuntia grafting

The cut top of an opuntia pad can also be used to bring on cactus seedlings more quickly.

Cut the roots off the seedlings, forming a flat base on each.

Place the seedling bases on the flat opuntia top and secure each one with a rubber band, as for normal grafting (see above).

When the seedlings are larger, re-graft or pot them.

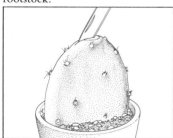

1 *Cut a slot in the top of the pad, using a sharp knife or a razor blade*

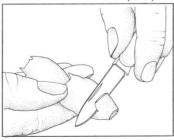

2 *Shape the scion into a wedge and insert it quickly into the slot*

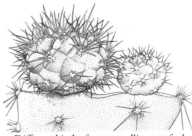

Different kinds of cactus seedlings grafted on to an opuntia pad can be left to grow into an unusual display

Greenhouse plants/1

Introduction

CYCLAMEN PERSICUM

Even a small greenhouse opens up vast new possibilities – from early vegetables to orchids. Equipment available can give complete, automatic control of cultivation

Greenhouses may be either heated or unheated. An unheated greenhouse will not keep out frost, but it creates warmer conditions for plants in the growing season. This extra heat speeds the ripening of crops, and improves the flowering of many decorative plants. An unheated greenhouse also protects plants from strong winds and rain and from attacks by birds, animals and some other pests.

Perhaps its most valuable function is to lengthen the growing season. Plants can be started into growth early in the spring, and either kept in the greenhouse or planted out in the garden. In the greenhouse, plants will grow on well into the autumn.

This artificial growing season is achieved in spring by the glass trapping the heat of the sun on clear days, and in autumn by retaining warmth which has built up in the soil and brickwork during summer.

Unheated greenhouses are widely used to grow a crop of tomatoes during spring and summer, and then for growing late-flowering chrysanthemums in autumn, when the tomato plants have been discarded. Many gardeners now also use them for grapes and melons.

For the gardener who is interested in obtaining the finest blooms, an unheated house is invaluable for growing a wide range of half-hardy shrubs, annuals, lilies, gladioli and many other bulbs.

All out-of-season vegetables normally grown under frames or cloches, such as lettuces, carrots, radishes, potatoes and French beans, can be grown just as well in an unheated greenhouse.

When artificial heat is introduced into a greenhouse, the range of plants that can be grown increases greatly, as tender plants which would never survive a British winter can be kept under perfect conditions.

By installing automatic equipment for heating, ventilation, shading and watering, environmental control is almost total.

Heated greenhouses are classified according to the minimum temperature maintained. A cool house is kept above 4°C (40°F) and a warm house above 13°C (55°F). Warm houses are now expensive to run because of fuel costs, and are not common.

A cool greenhouse is particularly useful for growing flowering plants from seeds or cuttings early in the year, to be planted in the garden at the beginning of summer.

How to choose a greenhouse

The first decision when buying a greenhouse, frame or cloche is whether to choose glass or plastic.

The main advantage of glass for greenhouses is that short-wave radiations from the sun pass through it easily, but once they are converted into long-wave heat radiations the glass becomes a barrier, and so the heat is retained inside the greenhouse.

Plastic takes in the rays but does not trap them, so that when the sun goes in the house cools down again very quickly.

Horticultural grades of polythene are available for greenhouses, and these last longer than ordinary plastic sheeting. Corrugated plastic should last about five years and is quite cheap to buy. A recently introduced acrylic plastic is very similar to glass, but is expensive.

Plastic scratches more easily than glass and the scratches become ingrained with dirt.

Condensation can also be a problem because whereas on glass the moisture forms a film, on plastic it collects, obscuring the light and causing drips. This difficulty can be overcome with the efficient use of fan ventilation.

However, for cloches and frames plastic is cheaper, easier to erect and gives excellent results where only temporary protection is needed.

Greenhouse plants/2

How to choose
a greenhouse

Greenhouse design
and shape

The different kinds
of framework

Greenhouse design and shape

There are three basic shapes of greenhouse: the vertical-sided, rectangular or square house; the sloping-sided house (known as the Dutch-light type); and the lean-to. Other shaped houses – round, dome-shaped and hexagonal – are also available. They are useful for displaying ornamental plants, but are not so practical for general greenhouse work or growing a selection of different plants.

A greenhouse with a sloping side or semi-circular roof captures more light and warmth because of the angle at which the glass is set to the sun's rays. The maximum amount of sunlight goes into the greenhouse, and the least is reflected, when the rays strike the glass at a right angle. The more acute the angle at which the rays strike, the more light is reflected and the less absorbed. However, sides that are too severely sloped will interfere with the greenhouse staging and tall plants. A greenhouse with glass sides down to ground level is the most versatile. Staging can be fitted, and it is possible to grow plants below it as well as on top. Such a greenhouse is ideal for tall-growing plants that need plenty of light, such as tomatoes, chrysanthemums and carnations.

Other greenhouses have a solid base of brick, concrete or wood.

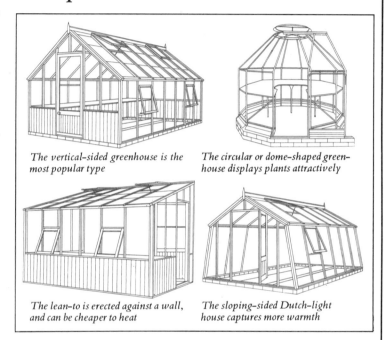

The vertical-sided greenhouse is the most popular type

The circular or dome-shaped greenhouse displays plants attractively

The lean-to is erected against a wall, and can be cheaper to heat

The sloping-sided Dutch-light house captures more warmth

Often there is sufficient light under the staging to grow shade-loving plants, or the area may be blacked out for forcing and blanching vegetables.

A lean-to can be more economical to heat than a free-standing greenhouse. If it is set against a brick wall facing south, the wall will act as a heat store, radiating warmth overnight after accumulating it during the day. However, a common fault of lean-to structures is that the roof does not slope enough. A flat roof collects the dirt, dead leaves and other debris.

The different kinds of framework

The framework of a greenhouse should have strength, durability and also an attractive appearance. Aluminium alloy, which may be stove-enamelled for a better appearance, is lightweight, strong, needs no painting and cannot warp or rot.

Galvanised iron is also strong, but needs painting occasionally to keep out rust. Painting is best done before glazing, and the framework should be examined every year for signs of wear and tear.

Various woods are used in greenhouse construction. Avoid the cheaper kinds, which have poor weather-resistance and will demand constant rot-proofing treatment. Red cedar lasts well, looks attractive, and is relatively inexpensive. Oak is sometimes used but can warp. Teak is excellent but often costly. Timber framework is available that holds the glass in slots, thus avoiding the use of putty and allowing easy glass removal for roof maintenance. Timber frames should be treated with wood preservatives or water repellents by the supplier before they are delivered.

Prefabricated greenhouses are available for erection by the buyer.

It is wise to buy base plinths of concrete, which are generally available as an extra.

With timber greenhouses, wooden base walls are usually supplied, but if brick or concrete walls are wanted, the purchaser will usually have to make them. Plans for such walls are supplied by the makers.

When the greenhouse is to be erected without a concrete plinth, the soil can be rammed firm and spread with shingle to make an excellent floor. The shingle, which looks neat, will hold moisture after damping down in summer, and therefore maintain humidity.

Greenhouse plants/3

What to look for when buying

Examine as many makers' catalogues as possible before buying. Give preference to a greenhouse as large as you can afford, not forgetting maintenance and heating. A greenhouse is so useful and fascinating that space soon becomes filled. If you intend to have staging on both sides of the greenhouse choose one 8 ft wide, to provide working space.

Some of the larger greenhouses have compartments with communicating doors. In this way different temperatures and conditions for a variety of plants can be maintained.

Strength of framework is always important, but especially in windy areas and when the roof is to be used to support hanging baskets of plants. Timber frames should be examined for knot holes ·which can cause weakness. A boarded base should be strong and thick. The roof should have an adequate slope to run condensation to one side.

Sliding doors are an advantage if they are well fitted. They cannot slam, are adjustable for extra ventilation and are space saving.

Most ventilators are still of the conventional hinged type. Louvred vents are a modern innovation, but some are not close shutting. Always make sure there are at least two ventilators, both side and top. Ideally there should be a side and top ventilator on each side of the house for every 4 ft of glass. They can then be used according to wind direction.

Where to site the greenhouse

A greenhouse should be given an open position where it receives all the light available. Never site a greenhouse next to trees. They cast shade, dirty the glass and can cause damage with falling branches.

Rising ground on the north or east side can shelter a site from cold winds.

It is convenient to have the greenhouse near the house, for easy access and to provide electricity and water.

A rectangular greenhouse is best sited so that its shorter sides face east and west. The longer sides, where the plants are growing, then capture more light in winter, and in summer probably will need shading only on the side facing south.

All these factors make for an ideal site. Lack of some, or even all of them, however, does not rule out the probability of success with a greenhouse. For example, if your only possible site is in almost constant shade, you could specialise in shade-loving plants.

Erecting the greenhouse
All prefabricated greenhouses are delivered with full instructions for erection. Even the larger ones can be put up with only one helper – some can even be erected single-handed. Level and firm the ground some time before erection, and if the greenhouse is larger than 8 ft × 6 ft, make a foundation for it. This need not be elaborate, especially if the house is mounted on concrete. One way of making a foundation is to dig out a shallow trench and fill it with very liquid concrete, which finds its own level by flowing. Any concrete foundation or base supplied with the greenhouse can then be set on this. However, a greenhouse with base walls of brick needs a base and foundation built by a professional. Glass is best handled when it is dry, but not cold. Painting is best done before the glass is put in.

Heating and heat conservation

In practice there is little difference between the costs of the various fuels. The greater efficiency of electricity, for instance, tends to balance out its slightly higher costs.

It is often more economical to use two fuels rather than one for heating. The cheaper, such as paraffin, is used for background warmth, and the dearer, such as electricity, is used to attain maximum heat with thermostatic control. Unfortunately thermostatic control is difficult on storage heaters that use off-peak electricity, making them unsuitable.

In an open position the winter sun can provide free warmth. A lean-to may be against a wall that will store outside warmth or warmth from the house, and maintain frost-free conditions overnight. Winds carry away heat, and in windy districts a windbreak of trees helps reduce fuel bills.

Many larger greenhouses can be divided into compartments with communicating doors, to provide different temperatures and conditions under the same roof. If there are three compartments, the coolest should be nearest the outside door, and the warmest in the centre.

Fit draught-excluding material to doors and ventilators if necessary.

Fuel used
The minimum safe temperature must be maintained during severe cold spells. Consequently, the amount of heat loss during the coldest conditions must be known, and heating equipment capable of compensating for it needs to be installed. Heat loss from all-glass greenhouses is given in the table below.

These figures assume an outside temperature of −7°C (19°F). They give the minimum output of heat needed in watts for electrical equipment and British Thermal Units per hour for oil, gas or solid fuel. The figures apply to all-glass greenhouses. For a house with brick or concrete base walls the figures will be lower. However, it is always safer to assume maximum heat losses.

If you have a greenhouse 6 ft × 10 ft, you will see that a heater with an output capable of 3580 watts or 12,200 BTU/hr is recommended if you want a winter minimum temperature of 13°C (55°F), even during very cold weather.

| Greenhouse size (ft) | Desired temperature (minimum) | | | | | |
| | 13°C (55°F) | | 7°C (45°F) | | 4°C (40°F) | |
	Watts	BTU/hr	Watts	BTU/hr	Watts	BTU/hr
5 × 6	2050	7000	1470	5000	1200	4000
6 × 6	2460	8400	1750	6000	1400	4800
6 × 8	2930	10,000	2500	7100	1700	5700
6 × 10	3580	12,200	2550	8750	2000	7000
6 × 14	4310	14,700	3100	10,500	2500	8400
8 × 8	3580	12,200	2550	8750	2000	7000
8 × 10	4000	13,650	2850	9750	2300	7800
8 × 12	4520	15,400	3250	11,000	2600	8800
8 × 14	4790	16,300	3400	11,600	2700	9300
10 × 10	5000	17,100	3600	12,250	2900	9800
10 × 15	6640	22,600	4750	16,100	3800	12,900
10 × 20	7920	27,600	5800	19,700	4700	15,800

Electricity – the most practical heating

The most efficient and useful form of heating for the average greenhouse is electricity.

It is most likely to be trouble-free, gives excellent automatic control, produces no harmful fumes and does not raise humidity in winter. There is no need to transport or store fuel, and equipment is usually compact.

If you intend to use electricity, have a permanent power supply installed by a qualified electrician.

For the amateur's greenhouse, the fan heater is the most popular. It is cheap to install – it plugs into a 13 amp waterproof socket – and is portable.

Fan heater

Fan heaters usually incorporate a thermostat which controls the fan and the heat output simultaneously.

The air circulation is good for the plants and reduces fungus diseases. A disadvantage is that if the fan breaks down, heat loss is total.

Tubular heater

Tubular heaters – aluminium tubes sealed at both ends and containing a heating element – are also highly efficient. They are screwed to the uprights around the sides of the greenhouse 7 in. clear of the floor and, if they are in banks, with an inch between the tubes. They are often sold in banks of three or four, but the heat distribution is better if they are fitted singly all round the greenhouse. They respond well to thermostatic control, and if one fails, the others should keep out the frost.

Convector heaters, which produce a current of warm air without a fan, are fairly inexpensive and easy to install, but heat distribution is not as good as with fan or tubular heaters. If you are using convectors, have one each end of the greenhouse.

Electric storage heaters, using off-peak electricity, are not really suitable because the heat output cannot be efficiently controlled.

Always use electrical equipment designed for the greenhouse. Domestic equipment is not satisfactory and can be dangerous.

For more economic use of electricity, soil-warming cables, used with air-warming, are invaluable.

Plants will not grow actively during the colder months unless they have a root temperature of 10–13°C (50–55°F). To maintain this by warming the air is very expensive, but cables warm the soil cheaply.

The cables are not expensive to buy and are easy to install. They are operated by mains electricity.

On an open bench for winter-flowering pot plants like cinerarias or calceolarias, the cables should be laid on 2 in. of sand, compost or soil and covered with another 1 in. of the same material.

In a greenhouse border, for tomatoes or other early salad crops, the cables should be buried 9 in. deep so that they will not be disturbed. For details of how to buy and install cables, see page 30.

To provide warm conditions for plants growing actively in cold months, sink pots into peat spread over soil-warming cables. Form a case with sheets of glass. Cables can also be laid 9 in. deep in a greenhouse border to provide warmth for tomatoes and other early crops

Paraffin, gas and hot-water systems

Paraffin heaters are cheaper to buy than electrical heaters, but running costs are about the same. The best kind to use are those that burn with a blue flame.

They produce a certain amount of carbon dioxide and water vapour, which can be beneficial to plants. It is important to use good-quality oil because low-grade oil, when burnt, can give off sulphur fumes which will damage plants. However, with modern paraffin heaters there is a flue which takes the fumes outside the greenhouse. The flue also reduces condensation in the greenhouse, which can harm the plants in winter.

Some paraffin heaters are fitted with an automatic temperature control, but the pilot flame burns continuously and may use the equivalent of 500 watts of electricity an hour, in addition to the fuel for heating.

Paraffin heaters are probably most useful as emergency heating during cold spells to supplement electrical heating, or during power cuts.

Hot-water pipes or natural gas heaters can be used for heating the greenhouse, but they are costly to install.

Aluminium hot-water pipes round the sides of the greenhouse, powered by a solid fuel, oil or gas-fired boiler are good for maintaining higher temperatures, but although they can be thermostatically controlled this is not really efficient. The pipes retain the heat and do not respond quickly to temperature changes.

Heaters that operate on natural gas are perfectly safe for plants, whereas coal gas is poisonous. For natural gas heating a properly installed supply is essential, and can be laid in the same trench as the electricity cable. However, unless the greenhouse is close to the house, this is costly. Natural gas heaters respond well to automatic control, so once installed are quite economical to run.

They are probably best for a lean-to greenhouse where the house itself is heated by gas central heating.

Thermostats

Most greenhouse heaters have a thermostat fitted, which regulates temperature to one or two degrees.

Electrical heating allows very accurate control, paraffin and gas slightly less. Hot-water systems are more difficult to control.

The thermostat should be easily adjustable and graduated in degrees. However, it is best set with a minimum/maximum thermometer placed separately in the greenhouse to record the highest and lowest temperatures since the previous day. The heater is adjusted so that the minimum temperature does not drop below the level required.

Greenhouse plants/5

Greenhouse staging
and shelving

Providing adequate
ventilation

Methods of shading
the greenhouse

Greenhouse staging and shelving

The simplest form of staging is the slatted wooden type. To provide humidity in summer, the staging should be covered with a 1 in. layer of moist sand resting on either polythene sheeting or on special sand trays. Pot plants standing on the sand will draw up moisture through their drainage holes by capillary action. The sand can be kept moist manually or automatically by one of the methods described opposite. In winter, when high humidity is not wanted, the sand should be cleared to allow good air circulation.

In greenhouses heated by hot-water pipes or electric heating tubes, it is sometimes possible to run these under that part of the staging used for propagation.

Oil or electric convection heaters

A covering of polythene and moist sand on the staging adds humidity

can also be put under the staging but care is obviously needed to avoid overheating: if you use these heaters, install asbestos or metal staging.

Shelving provides extra room for pots and trailing plants

Shelves above the staging can be used to provide extra room for pots or seed trays, and to accommodate trailing plants.

Providing adequate ventilation

A greenhouse needs at least two ventilators in the roof and some low-positioned ventilators at the side, otherwise it is likely to become too hot in summer. When top vents and side vents are open at the same time a rapid change of air takes place.

Sliding side vents also allow access to the area under staging, for cultivation and the addition or removal of pots or boxes. Top vents, and sometimes side vents, can be fitted with automatic openers. A compound inside the units expands or contracts with temperature changes and motivates a piston system of levers.

An alternative form of ventilation is by an electric extractor fan controlled by a thermostat. The fan is best placed in the apex of the roof, at the end of the greenhouse opposite the door. Various sizes of fan are

Automatic openers are available for top, and some side, vents. Sliding side vents help to regulate the temperatures inside the greenhouse

available. As the fan sucks air out of the greenhouse, sufficient air will usually come in under the door and through gaps under the glass. But

during very hot weather the door or vents at a distant point from the fan should be left open to give maximum ventilation.

Methods of shading the greenhouse

The most efficient method of shading the greenhouse is to use one of the proprietary roller blinds usually made of wood or plastic slats, or woven material such as hessian. These can be lowered on sunny days and rolled back on dull days. They can be fitted to the inside or outside of the roof, and should be set on rails a few inches from the glass.

Automatic blinds are also available but are expensive. Photo-electric cells operate exterior blinds.

An effective, and also cheaper, alternative to blinds is electrostatic shading paint. A concentrate is diluted in water and brushed or sprayed on the outside of the glass. It is waterproof, but will wipe off.

Blinds are usually used only on the greenhouse roof, although they are available to cover the sides as

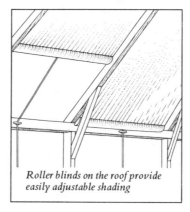

Roller blinds on the roof provide easily adjustable shading

well. A house where the ends face east and west should be shaded on the south side of the roof, one running north and south on both sides.

Electrostatic shading paint cannot be washed off by rain

Electrostatic paint can be applied on the side as well as the roof. If the greenhouse runs north-south paint the south, east, west sides, and roof.

A water supply in the greenhouse

Unless a greenhouse is being erected alongside an existing garden tap, a permanent water supply should be installed. This is work for a plumber, but the expense is justified by the saving in work and time later.

Once a tap has been provided, plants can be watered either by hand, with a hose or automatically.

Automatic watering has several advantages. It is more reliable than hand watering and promotes steady growth of plants. It saves time and enables you to leave the greenhouse unattended for days, or even weeks if suitable equipment is used.

The capillary sand bench is a popular method of automatic watering. Small units are available that can be extended. A unit consists of a plastic tray, a tank or reservoir, and a constant-level float valve.

A layer of sand is placed in the tray according to the supplier's recommendations. Mix the sand with a proprietary non-toxic algicide formulated to prevent the growth of algae. An alternative to sand is a proprietary absorbent mat.

The float valve regulates the level of water in the tray and hence the degree of wetness of the sand.

Use plastic pots with large drainage holes for capillary-bench work. Do not put crocks in when potting.

After potting the plants, press the pots down firmly on the moist sand or matting, so that the compost makes contact with it through the pots' drainage holes.

Water the pots well. This will ensure continued uptake of water from the capillary bench.

Another form of watering is trickle irrigation. This consists of a plastic pipeline with nozzles at intervals which drip water into the pots. The flow of water is usually controlled by a small water tank that siphons over automatically at intervals. The frequency and amount of water supplied is controlled by a valve that has to be adjusted by hand.

This method should not be used for plants which need only occasional and minimal watering, such as cacti.

Nozzles can be held over the pots by wire staples.

The lines can also be used to irrigate sand benches or matting.

A pipeline with misting jets can be fixed permanently over or under staging to provide overhead watering or damping down.

A modern method of automatic watering is by photo-electric control. A photo-electric cell automatically switches on a water valve when the light reaches a certain intensity. The water then runs for a set period. This method can be used to control capillary benches, trickle irrigation and overhead irrigation.

If you find it difficult to know when to water plants a soil-moisture meter is invaluable. It consists of a dial fixed to a long probe. The probe is inserted into the compost in the pot. The dial is calibrated to give 'dry', 'moist' and 'wet' readings. The best meters are also numbered, and have a guide to which numbers are suitable for the various plants.

Capillary bench and moisture meter *The tray of sand is watered by a tank, and pots draw up moisture from the sand. The moisture meter in the pot shows when to water*

Trickle irrigation *Nozzles on a plastic pipeline drip water on to the compost in pots. Water flow is controlled by a small tank*

Other useful fittings for the greenhouse

There are other fittings that, although not essential, are useful accessories in a greenhouse.

For example, guttering can be fitted to the greenhouse roof to run off rain water. This can be collected in an outside or internal water butt by means of a downpipe, and used for watering plants. A supply of rain water is useful for watering lime-hating plants in hard-water areas.

Ensure that an outside butt used for this purpose is covered by a lid to prevent dirt entering. The pipe from the roof should be covered with gauze to trap any debris.

A soil thermometer measures the temperature of soil or compost heated by cables in a propagator, garden frame or greenhouse bed. In a propagating case soil temperatures will need to reach up to 18°C

(64°F) for growing plants from seeds and cuttings. Garden frames and greenhouse borders require a winter soil temperature of 10–13°C (50–55°F) for early salad crops.

Artificial lighting is useful for working during dark winter evenings. Moisture-proof electric fittings are available for the greenhouse and should always be installed by a qualified electrician.

Propagators and their uses

A propagator is a box with a transparent cover, which is used for germinating seeds or rooting cuttings. It can be either unheated or heated.

An unheated propagator merely provides a sealed humid environment for cuttings or seeds. A heated propagator also provides bottom heat, which makes rooting and germination more certain. Many storage organs, such as bulbs, corms, rhizomes and tubers, also start into growth earlier if given a little extra warmth.

With large propagators young plants can be kept inside until they are well established. A large unit can also be used as a permanent home for small tropical plants, saving the cost of heating the whole greenhouse to a high temperature.

There are many kinds of propagator. Most are heated by electricity using soil-warming cables. Other propagators using paraffin heaters are less efficient.

The simplest units take one or two seed trays. They can be bought with a heating element fitted into the base and are simply plugged into the mains electricity supply. The trays stand on a layer of sand or gravel. More elaborate versions will take a range of pots and boxes and are thermostatically controlled.

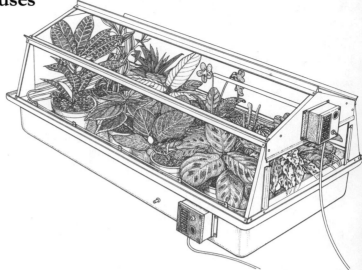

A large heated propagator can be used to house a collection of small tropical plants, saving the cost of heating the whole greenhouse

You can make your own propagating case or bench, with a piece of asbestos sheeting slightly narrower than the greenhouse staging and cut to the length you require – 5 ft is a useful size. The asbestos forms a base to stand on the staging, and pieces of board, 9 in. high, are fixed round the sides to make a box. The asbestos sheet can be put directly on to the metal staging supports, saving the cost of the normal top. If this is done the asbestos will need to be supported with wooden or metal cross pieces. Cut three or four drainage holes in the asbestos and spread a 2 in. layer of sand on it. Lay soil-warming cables on this, and cover with a 3 in. layer of moist sand, or 1 in. of sand and 3 in. of peat.

How to buy and install soil-warming cables

Cuttings root slowly if the soil is cold, and seeds are slow to germinate in cold composts. To heat the soil or compost in a propagator or garden frame by air warmth would be slow and costly. And a high air temperature in winter or spring would tend to produce unwanted top growth in plants being propagated. The simple and economical answer is to use soil-warming cables.

Cables are made in lengths to fit any area and give the correct amount of heat.

To grow early melons or marrows in an outside frame, 5 watts of electricity per square foot will be needed to heat the soil to about 10°C (50°F). For seeds and cuttings in a greenhouse propagator, 15 watts per square foot will give a soil temperature of 18°C (64°F).

The following table shows the wattage and length of cable needed to heat any given area to a soil temperature of 18°C (64°F).

Cables are available with a thermostat fitted for economical control of the heat. The wire is fully insulated and usually has a braided metal earthed sleeve for safety. The heating section is usually a distinctive colour and must not be cut.

Cables can be connected direct to the mains supply, or special low-voltage cables can be operated from a transformer – which is safer if there is a risk of damage to cables from garden tools.

All mains electrical work should be done by qualified electricians.

Always buy the correct length to fit the area to be heated. Put a 2 in. layer of sand on the base of the propagator and put the cable on this. Lay it backwards and forwards over the whole area to be heated. Avoid sharp bends and lay the cable not less than 4 in. and not more than 8 in. apart. It must never be allowed to cross itself or any adjacent cables. Cover with a further 1 in. of sand and 3 in. of moist peat. Cuttings can be planted directly into the peat, and pots can be sunk in it so that each base is in contact with the sand.

For air warming alone, or in addition to soil warming, cables can be fastened to woodwork around the sides of the frame.

Area (sq. ft)	Wattage	Cable length (ft)
Up to 6	75	20
12	150	40
25	300	80
50	600	160
100	1200	320
150	1750	470
200	2500	693

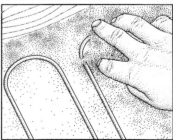

1 *Spread a layer of sand on the base of the case and lay the cable on it*

2 *Cover the cable with sand and moist peat to distribute the heat evenly*

Providing the right conditions for plants

Watering, humidity, temperature, shading and feeding can be controlled in the greenhouse to suit almost any kind of plant.

Watering If compost is waterlogged, the roots of the plants rot. Aim for a compost that is just moist. It is always better to be sparing rather than generous with water.

In autumn and winter, when plants are dormant or growing slowly, very little water is required. In spring and summer, when plants are growing strongly, water can be given freely. The amount depends on the size of the plants, their speed of growth, and whether they are bearing fruit or flowering freely. When the weather is cool and daylight poor, plants need far less water than when the temperature is high and conditions are bright.

Generally the best time to water is in the morning. This avoids creating excess moisture at the roots at night, when plants cannot use it, and keeps down overnight humidity.

Always use clean water. If soft water is required for lime-hating plants, collect rain water in a butt, with a lid on it to keep out dirt and leaves.

In warm weather, greenhouse plants benefit from overhead spraying with water. This cleans the foliage, enabling it to breathe.

Humidity and damping down Humidity is the moisture-content of the air. It is increased by spraying plants with water, or by damping down – drenching the walls, floor and staging of the greenhouse (but keeping water off plants with velvety or hairy foliage). The presence of a damp surface, such as a capillary bench, will also raise humidity. Humidity is lowered by watering sparingly and confining water to the area of the plant roots, and by increasing ventilation.

In summer high humidity is usually beneficial to most plants. It reduces the amount of water that foliage loses through transpiration and that compost loses through evaporation. Many popular greenhouse pot plants benefit, in a hot, dry summer, if the greenhouse is damped down at least twice a day, in the morning and evening. However, provided the plants are regularly watered and maximum ventilation given, no popular and 'easy' plant should fail.

In winter, humidity should be kept down; ventilate the greenhouse whenever outside temperature will allow, and water only lightly. High humidity in cold weather creates condensation on the glass (which reduces light), the possibility of fungus diseases and the danger from dripping and waterlogged compost.

To keep down humidity in winter, allow capillary watering systems to dry out.

Temperature This should be controlled to suit the type of plants grown. In summer, temperature is reduced by damping down, ventilation and shading.

Damping down has a cooling effect because heat is absorbed as the water evaporates, but this will not happen without ventilation. There should be at least two ventilators top and bottom on each side of the house, and in very hot weather the door can be opened.

Shading There are two main reasons for shading a greenhouse.

First, many tropical plants originate from forest areas and thrive best in partially shaded sites.

Second, few plants, however tropical in origin, require a temperature above 29°C (85°F), and for most 24°C (75°F) is adequate. Temperatures above 32°C (90°F) can harm many plants. In warm sunny weather, it is difficult in the average small greenhouse to keep temperatures down with ventilation alone, and shading must also be used.

If possible, shading should be graduated from heavy (an overall solid layer of shading paint) to light (wavy lines in stripes with a space between each line, or sprayed dots), to provide different light requirements for different plants. For example, most cacti need either no shade at all or a very light cover, whereas most ferns need full shade during the brightest, warmest weather. Slatted blinds can be rolled down completely or partially, depending on the amount of sunlight. If shading cannot be graduated, shade-loving plants can be grown under staging or climbing plants.

In general, a part of a greenhouse used for propagation will need shading from mid-March to mid-October. For growing pot plants, shading from mid-April to late September will be adequate.

After winter, plants are often sensitive to a sudden temperature rise caused by sunny spells which, even in cold weather, can make the greenhouse extremely warm. For this reason, light shading may be necessary in spring.

Feeding Overfeeding, like overwatering, is often responsible for the death of pot plants. A build-up of nutrient salts in the compost can damage plant roots. If the correct potting and seed composts are used, plants will need no feeding until they are well established and the pots are filled with roots.

As with watering, feeding must be regulated according to the plants' needs. Fast-growing, heavily cropping plants such as tomatoes, cucumbers or chrysanthemums, can be fed generously. Slow-growing plants such as rock plants and many cacti, can be ruined by excessive feeding.

Plants absorb nutrients only in solution. For this reason, liquid feeds are best because they are rapid in action and effective. High fertiliser concentrations can damage plants, so never give dry feeds at the roots.

Use properly balanced proprietary pot-plant or greenhouse-plant feeds.

Do not add dried blood, ammonium sulphate or bonemeal to pot plants in a hit-or-miss way. Epsom Salts (magnesium sulphate) can be used to help correct magnesium deficiency in plants prone to it, such as tomatoes and *Solanum capsicastrum*. If the leaves are pale, with yellow margins later becoming brown, and the plant is stunted, water or spray the plants a few times with a solution of $\frac{1}{2}$–1 oz. ($\frac{1}{2}$–1 tablespoon) of salts per gallon of water.

Foliar feeds are now sold for plants that need a quick boost to growth or whose root action is slow, such as young, newly transplanted plants.

Plants long established in pots can be given a top dressing of John Innes base fertiliser incorporated with the top couple of inches of compost.

Before going on holiday A greenhouse can usually be left to look after itself for a day – although in summer take care to attend to watering and shading each morning if you are not returning until evening. For periods of a week or more try to get a friend or neighbour to help.

If there is no one to help, automatic equipment is the ideal answer (pp. 28-29). Most automatic watering systems cope for at least a week without attention.

However, if you cannot afford automatic equipment the only thing to do is to carry out the following jobs before going on a summer holiday. Water as thoroughly as possible before leaving. Provide humidity by covering the plants with clear polythene sheeting or bags. If you are not using polythene, thoroughly damp down the greenhouse and leave some pans or baths filled with water inside to maintain humidity.

Completely shade the greenhouse. Leave plenty of ventilation, but reduce vents on the same side as the prevailing wind. Check for pests and diseases, and give routine treatment with systemic pesticides and fungicides if necessary. Remove any flowers and buds about to mature. Do any outstanding potting-on or pricking out. Gather any fruit or vegetables almost ready for cropping.

Greenhouse plants/8

Watering

Humidity and damping down

Temperature

Shading

Feeding

Keeping greenhouse and equipment clean

Cleanliness is vital for success in the greenhouse. It reduces pests and diseases and encourages general plant vigour and health. Keep all pots and containers clean. Try to use equipment made of plastic, metal or glass, which cannot harbour disease organisms.

Regularly wash grime and algae from both sides of the greenhouse glass. Wash down staging and interior structures, using clean water with detergent. Proprietary algicides are also available to keep greenhouse floors, benches and the various forms of automatic watering systems free from slimes and algae.

In an empty house, with no risk of fumes damaging plants, a sterilant such as Jeyes Fluid can be added to the water before washing down.

In areas with hard water, deposits of lime will often form on watering equipment, impairing its efficiency.

To remove these, use a diluted solution of a proprietary kettle descaler or bath stain remover containing formic acid. This can also be used for cleaning grimy glass.

The greenhouse should not be used to store garden tools or other equipment. These harbour pests. Regularly inspect plants and remove any dead flowers or decaying foliage. Isolate unhealthy plants by taking them out of the greenhouse or putting them in a polythene bag. Use only sterilised composts.

Fumigation is an easy and efficient method of killing pests. It should be done twice a year, in October and March. Certain pesticides sold for spraying, such as malathion and BHC, are also available to be used as fumigants.

Before fumigation, water plants but keep foliage dry. Do not carry out the operation in strong sunlight and when temperatures are high. It is best done in the evening, after which the greenhouse should be kept completely shut until morning, and then should be ventilated freely.

To keep fumes and vapours in the greenhouse, block any gaps with wet sacking or masking tape. Do not fumigate on a windy day.

To give the recommended amount of fumigation, it is necessary to know the cubic capacity of the greenhouse. This is ascertained by multiplying width by length and by average height.

If the greenhouse has contained plants badly infected by disease, sterilise the empty house by burning sulphur at the rate of 1 lb. per 1000 cu. ft. The sulphur is ignited with wood shavings to burn with a blue flame. The sulphur dioxide produced is poisonous and will kill all plants. It must not be inhaled.

The correct way to pot your plants

Plastic pots have generally replaced clay ones, because they are easy to clean, lightweight and not so easily broken. Also, as they are non-porous, less watering is needed.

When pot plants have to be plunged in moist peat or sand, however, clay is preferable, as it allows moisture to pass through the pot to the roots. Plants that prefer dry growing conditions also do better in clay pots.

The most popular sizes for general greenhouse use are 2½ in. (for seedlings), 3½ in. and 5 in. (all measurements refer to the inside diameter of the top of the pot). Large plants, shrubs and climbers may need correspondingly larger pots. Ensure that all pots have adequate drainage holes.

For short plants such as rock plants, some succulents, and small bulbs, half-pots or seed pans can be used, which are only half the depth of normal pots. They give a better balanced appearance to the potted plant and use less compost. Before use, all pots should be scrupulously clean. Scrub them thoroughly, if necessary, to remove any dirt and encrustations.

Thoroughly soak the clay pots, especially new ones. Otherwise they will dry out the compost.

Plastic pots need no drainage material in the bottom. Clay pots up to 5 in. need no drainage material either, but if you are potting a plant in a clay pot larger than 5 in., first cover the drainage hole with a few pieces of broken pot or clean pebbles. Even this should not be done if the pots are to be stood on a capillary sand bench.

To pot a plant, place moist potting compost in the pot and tap it down gently on the bench. Hold the plant in the pot so that the roots are resting on the compost, and the base of the plant comes to about 1 in. below the top rim of the pot.

Position the plant centrally and run more compost around it, leaving 1 in. between the top of the compost and the top of the pot. Always take care not to damage the roots. A few taps of the pot on the bench will be sufficient to anchor them firmly. Do not firm the compost with the fingers, as this may cause it to become waterlogged.

After potting, water the plant. Be careful not to water too much. If roots have been damaged, they may rot if the compost is excessively wet. It is usually sufficient to fill the space on top of the compost and allow the water to drain through.

1 Place drainage material in the base of a clay pot larger than 5 in.

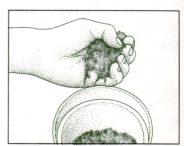

2 Put moist potting compost into the pot and tap it down gently

3 Position the plant centrally, add more compost and tap the pot on the bench

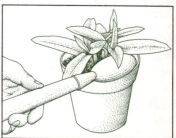

4 After potting, water by filling the 1 in. space between rim and compost

Potting on growing plants

Developing plants are potted on into a larger pot each time their roots fill their present pot.

When roots appear through the drainage holes, turn the pot upside-down, allowing the plant's stem to pass between the fingers. Tap the rim with a stick or on the edge of the bench to loosen the root ball; if the plant is well established, it should come away cleanly.

The new pot should provide 1 in. extra space all round the root ball. Position the plant centrally and fill in compost round it. Consolidate the compost by tapping the pot on the bench a few times, then level the surface with the fingers. If the gap is too narrow for the fingers, use a potting stick. Leave a 1 in. space at the top for watering.

1 *Turn the pot upside-down and tap the rim to release the root ball*

2 *The root ball should come away quite easily if the plant is well rooted*

3 *Replant in a pot larger in diameter than the old pot*

Potting composts and seed composts

Never use ordinary garden soil for growing plants and sowing seeds in containers. Always use good potting and seed composts which have been partially sterilised to destroy pests, diseases and weed seeds.

There are many proprietary seed and potting composts sold, some based on loam and some on peat or a mixture of peat and sand. Loam-based compost is not difficult to make. If you need large quantities, making it yourself is cheaper.

For mixing small batches of compost, and also for carrying out potting and seed-sowing operations, a potting bench is needed. This consists of a tray with two sides and a back, which can be put on the greenhouse staging. It should have a smooth surface that can be kept clean and sterile, such as plastic-covered wood or sheet aluminium.

The John Innes composts have been successfully used for many years. Their composition is:

John Innes seed compost

	Parts by volume
Sterilised loam	2
Peat	1
Coarse sand	1

To each bushel add 1½ oz. of superphosphate of lime and ¾ oz. of ground chalk or limestone.

John Innes No. 1 potting compost

	Parts by volume
Sterilised loam	7
Peat	3
Coarse sand	2

To each bushel add ¼ lb. of John Innes base fertiliser and ¾ oz. of ground chalk or limestone.

John Innes base fertiliser

	Parts by weight
Hoof and horn	2
Superphosphate of lime	2
Sulphate of potash	1

A bushel is the amount that will fit into a box 22 in. × 10 in. × 10 in. without compacting.

Ideally, the loam used in these composts should be medium-to-heavy texture loam from the top spit of good meadow land. Turves should be stacked grass-side downwards in heaps up to 5 ft high, with layers of farmyard manure at 12 in. intervals, and left for at least six months before use.

A good-quality baled moss peat must be used and clean horticultural grit or sand. Sterilisation is not necessary for the peat and sand.

The amount of fertiliser and chalk added to the potting compost can be doubled to give John Innes No. 2, and trebled to give John Innes No. 3. For most purposes the No. 2 compost will be found suitable. Slow-growing plants can be given No. 1, but fast and vigorous subjects, such as tomatoes and chrysanthemums, need No. 3. Fertiliser concentrations above this are usually unnecessary. John Innes base fertiliser can also be used as a top dressing.

Loam-free composts Because the top-quality loam used in John Innes compost is now in short supply, loamless all-peat or peat-and-sand composts have been developed.

Plants tend to grow very quickly initially in all-peat composts and seed germination is good. However, a disadvantage is that the peat is light-weight and large plants tend to become top-heavy. They may topple over, particularly if they are in plastic pots. A large pot plant is probably best planted in a soil-based compost, especially if it will need staking.

All composts composed largely of peat tend to dry out more slowly in dull weather, yet lose moisture more rapidly when it is sunny. They need to be kept rather wetter than soil-based composts so that the plants can draw up moisture.

However, avoid over-watering which can cause the peat to become waterlogged. Water peat-based compost little and often. Another cause of waterlogging can be tightly packed compost.

How to pot large greenhouse bulbs

When potting large greenhouse bulbs such as hippeastrum (often sold as amaryllis) allow at least a third of the bulb to protrude above the surface of the compost in a 5–6 in. pot. This places the bulb at the right height to provide sufficient room in the pot for root growth.

After greenhouse bulbs have been potted, they should be left in the greenhouse and watered sparingly. Hippeastrum and lachenalia can be gently forced to provide earlier flowers. These two bulbs often make plenty of top growth before rooting, which takes place only as the leaves begin to develop; and they may even flower before making new roots, as in the case of hippeastrum. For this reason take great care when the plants are moved about in case insufficient roots have formed to anchor the plant.

How to sterilise compost ingredients

Only loam and leaf-mould need to be sterilised. Never use composts twice, and never sterilise a fully made-up compost containing fertilisers. The materials to be sterilised must be reasonably dry.

Leaf-mould is sterilised by pouring on boiling water, and then draining. Loam should be sterilised separately, and not in the presence of leaf-mould or fertiliser.

Various proprietary sterilising chemicals are on the market. However, the best method is steam sterilisation: the loam can be used very soon afterwards, there is no risk of damage to plants from fumes, and the method is effective.

Small electric sterilisers can be bought quite cheaply. They work on the principle of steam from boiling water passing through the material that is to be sterilised.

Water is poured into the boiling compartment of the steriliser, to the level recommended by the manufacturer.

The dry loam is first sifted to free it from lumps, then placed into the bin of the steriliser, which has a perforated bottom.

The sterilising bin is placed on top of the boiling compartment and steam is passed through the loam until the temperature at the top reaches 82°C (180°F). This should be maintained for about ten minutes but must not exceed 93°C (200°F), or beneficial soil organisms will be killed. Best results are obtained when the top temperatures are reached within about 40 minutes.

After sterilising the loam, tip it out on to a clean surface to cool down. It can be used immediately, if necessary.

Small quantities of loam can be sterilised by the same method, using a kitchen steamer.

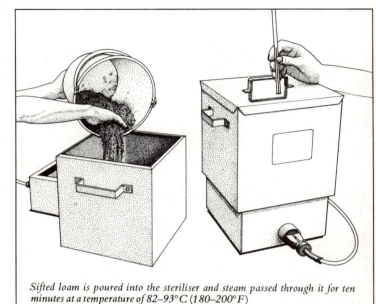

Sifted loam is poured into the steriliser and steam passed through it for ten minutes at a temperature of 82–93°C (180–200°F)

How to mix your own composts

Do not make a large amount of compost – it is difficult to mix.

Spread out the measured peat, sterilised loam and sand on the potting bench. Put a little of the sand in a bucket.

Weigh the fertilisers with a small kitchen balance that measures to fractions of an ounce.

Mix the fertilisers with the sand in the bucket. Then spread the basic ingredients in layers over the potting bench and add the fertiliser-and-sand mixture, sprinkling it evenly over the surface.

Finally, mix all the ingredients really thoroughly.

Special composts
There are a few plants, such as orchids for which special composts are needed.

For plants preferring an acid soil or compost, such as ericas, callunas, and rhododendrons, omit the chalk from both the John Innes potting and seed composts.

Proprietary acid, or ericaceous, composts can be bought.

The addition of sterilised leaf-mould helps plants that grow naturally in woodland soils, such as lilies. Apart from this, it is better not to add anything to the standard compost formulae.

All the composts must be used damp, but never waterlogged. They should be stored in clean, closed containers and not left exposed to the air, which may introduce pests, diseases and weed seeds.

Use compost as soon as possible after buying or preparing it. Compost must not be re-used but can be incorporated in the garden to improve the texture of the soil.

1 *Spread out the measured peat, loam and sand on the potting bench*

2 *Weigh out the fertilisers and mix them with a little sand in a bucket*

3 *Sprinkle the mixture of fertiliser and sand over the basic ingredients*

4 *After adding the fertiliser and sand, mix all the ingredients thoroughly*

Selecting plants

By taking care over the individual plants' lighting, heating or humidity requirements, and by fitting a greenhouse with compartments or accommodating smaller plants in propagating cases, a surprisingly varied selection of plants can be grown successfully in one greenhouse.

Even so, you will make things easier for yourself if you avoid combinations involving plants with very different requirements, for example, cacti and ferns.

It is best to keep members of the following groups of plants in separate sections of the greenhouse: fruit and vines; vegetables and salad crops; plants to be propagated; specialist plants such as chrysanthemums and alpines; and decorative plants. And for good show or exhibition results, the crop or flowers should be given a greenhouse of their own. The right conditions and pest and disease control can then be maintained without having to worry about any other plants.

Try to choose decorative plants that provide year-round interest (see pp. 44-46).

A succession of plants

In an unheated greenhouse, a succession of plants with different growing periods can be grown through the year. For example, climbing French beans can be sown in the greenhouse border in February for cropping in April and May; these can be followed by tomato plants when the beans are cleared; and late-flowering chrysanthemums can be brought in when the tomatoes are finished.

An unheated greenhouse can be used to shelter practically all the favourite outdoor ornamental plants from spring to autumn. But remember that the purpose of the unheated house is to give weather protection only, so always provide maximum ventilation and just enough shading to prevent sun scorch. Special favourites for a house of this kind are plants giving flowers for cutting and for flower shows: for example, roses, border carnations, sweet peas, dahlias, bulbs of most kinds and gladioli.

An unheated house can also be used in winter to protect hardy plants that are difficult or susceptible to damage by excessive wet, such as *Lobelia cardinalis*, some agapanthus varieties, many rock plants, and not quite hardy bulbs.

Another use is the protection of early-flowering hardy shrubs, such as camellias, grown in pots.

Annuals with alpines

A greenhouse devoted entirely to alpines, with airy and bright conditions, is also excellent for summer-flowering annuals. Many of the ordinary garden annuals will give remarkable results grown in an alpine house in pots of good compost. After the alpines flower in spring, they can be put in frames outside for the summer to give more space inside the greenhouse for the annuals.

A cool greenhouse – kept at a minimum of 4–7°C (40–45°F) in winter – is commonly used for saving plants such as pelargoniums and fuchsias. In early spring it can be used to display such plants as calceolarias, cinerarias, primulas, schizanthus and salpiglossis, grown on from the previous autumn's sowings. Bulbs can be brought in at this time for forcing.

In the spring, when summer-flowering plants such as pelargoniums and fuchsias are coming to life, you can also start many summer-flowering bulbs such as sinningias (gloxinias), smithianthas, gloriosas, achimenes and lilies.

For giving a winter display, perpetual-flowering carnations, gerberas, zonal pelargoniums, browallias and some fibrous begonias are invaluable. Space under the staging can be used in winter for forcing rhubarb, endives and chicory.

In warmer conditions – a winter temperature of 13°C (55°F) – gloxinias, streptocarpus, saintpaulias, columneas and achimenes grow well together and provide winter blooms as well as additional colour. With an even higher temperature, 16°C (61°F) in winter, a great range of subtropical and tropical foliage plants can be grown together.

There are many beautiful shrubs and perennials for the greenhouse, and many greenhouse species will allow vigorous pruning to keep them compact.

House-plant shops are excellent sources of greenhouse plants, and most house plants are at their best after being kept under glass. Some will flower and even fruit in a greenhouse.

Growing plants in hanging containers

Trailing plants are best displayed in hanging containers, which can be fixed to the greenhouse roof or walls. Some cheaper, ready-made greenhouses will not take the weight of large baskets, but small pots should be quite safe.

The old-fashioned wire basket is now covered with plastic to prevent rusting. Ordinary plastic pots can also be used. Drill holes round the rim of the pot and pass wires through.

First line the baskets with sphagnum moss or black plastic sheeting. Then fill the basket with potting compost and put in the plants evenly around the edge. Pierce holes in plastic sheeting to take each plant's roots. Hanging containers dry out quicker than ordinary pots in dry weather, and need a daily soaking.

Plants effective in baskets include pendulous begonias, ivy-leaved pelargoniums, fuchsias, nasturtiums, lobelias and tradescantias.

Sometimes bulbs, such as lachenalia, are pushed between the meshes and through the moss. They will grow out in a ball-like mass of bloom.

1 *Line a hanging basket with sphagnum moss to contain the compost*

2 *Fill the basket with potting compost and put in the plants*

Seeds: the cheapest way for a mass of bloom

Growing from seed is a cheap and easy way of stocking a greenhouse and filling it with colour all year round. Buy seed from a reputable firm and sow at the earliest correct time. Do not sow old seed, which may have deteriorated.

Use 5 in. pots or seed pans or small plastic seed trays. Half fill each with slightly moist seed compost. Before sowing very fine seed, sprinkle the surface with a little seed compost rubbed through a fine sieve. Gently level and firm the surface.

Sow the seed as thinly and evenly as possible by tapping it out of the packet with the forefinger. More even distribution can be attained if very fine seed is mixed with a little fine silver sand before sowing. If seed is known to take six months or more to germinate, incorporate a fungicidal seed dressing with it, to prevent it rotting in the compost.

Many seeds are now available in pelleted form. A coating increases their size, and enables you to space them accurately.

After sowing, cover the seed with about its own depth of sifted compost. Do not cover excessively, since the seed needs air for germination and the emerging seedling needs light and air to develop sturdily right from the start. Do not cover very fine seeds or those that germinate best if exposed to the light, such as sinningias (gloxinia), streptocarpus, smithianthas and saintpaulias. Spray the compost with a fine mist until it is thoroughly moist.

Label each seed tray with a waterproof plastic label.

To keep the compost moist, cover the seed trays with a sheet of glass or plastic. But first cover the tray with a piece of absorbent white paper to prevent condensation dripping back on to the seed. The paper allows some light through if seeds need it.

For satisfactory germination the seed must have a suitable temperature. The seeds of most greenhouse plants will germinate well at 13–18°C (55–64°F). The more tender the plants, the higher the temperature required. Warm-greenhouse plants may need 18–24°C (64–75°F). If the temperature in the greenhouse is not high enough – perhaps in early spring – put the seed tray in a heated propagator.

Seed varies considerably in the time it takes to germinate, so never discard seed that appears to have failed before giving it plenty of time to break and produce roots.

Pricking out As soon as the two seed leaves appear on each seedling, the seedlings must be pricked out. Transfer the seedlings individually

to 2½ in. pots of John Innes No. 1 potting compost or in a group to large seed trays (8½ in. × 14 in.).

Many slow-growing greenhouse pot plants are best put in seed trays first, as trays do not dry out as quickly as small pots. Set seedlings 1–2 in. apart, according to their size. As a precaution against damping-off disease, water in with Cheshunt Compound, diluted according to the maker's instructions. After pricking out, the seedlings need a well-lit part of the greenhouse, but not excessive sunlight.

Pot on greenhouse-plant seedlings into 3½ in. pots when the pots are filled with roots, or when seedlings in boxes touch each other.

Plants for bedding out in the garden need hardening off.

1 *Sow the seed thinly on moist seed compost in pots or small trays*

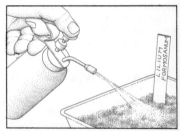

2 *After covering seed with compost, label it and spray with water*

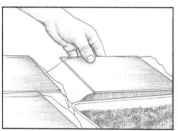

3 *Cover tray with paper, to absorb the condensation, then a sheet of glass*

4 *Immediately leaves appear, prick out the seedlings to pots or trays of compost*

Bulbous-rooting plants for early flowers

Many greenhouse plants are grown from storage organs – bulbs, tubers, corms and rhizomes. For early results, they are best started in 3–5°C (5–10°F) more heat than their normal growing temperature. Examples include hippeastrums, tuberous begonias, gloriosas, achimenes, smithianthas, sinningias (gloxinias), gesnerias, and many of the summer-flowering bulbs and corms that can be started in late winter or early spring for early flowers.

Most bulbs can be potted direct into pots and then placed in a warm propagator. However, it is not always easy to see on tubers, corms and rhizomes which end should be

uppermost, and they should first be immersed in moist peat in a suitable container placed in a warm propagator or on the greenhouse bench. Inspect them every few days, and when shoots or roots are visible take them out of the propagator and pot them the correct way up in potting compost. Gloxinias and begonias, in particular, should be treated in this way.

In autumn, after the foliage has begun to fade, allow plants from bulbs and other storage organs to go dry. When the pots are quite dry, tip out the contents and separate the bulbs from the compost. Clean away any compost and remove any

dead roots. Store the bulbs in dry sand in a frost-free, dry place. If the greenhouse becomes damp in winter, store somewhere else.

Do not tip out and clean plants with fragile tubers or rhizomes, such as gloriosas and smithianthas, as they can be damaged.

They are best left in their pots, which should be set on their side, to avoid accidental watering, in a dry, frost-free place.

They should be removed from their pots and repotted in fresh compost just before they are due to restart into growth. In most cases they will have multiplied. Divide up and pot the pieces separately.

How to increase your greenhouse plants

There are several simple ways of growing new greenhouse plants from existing ones, and some plants respond to one method better than another. However, softwood cuttings and division are the easiest methods. They also produce new plants identical to the parent plant.

In all cases, make sure that you propagate only from completely healthy plants. Never use plants with yellow or mottled foliage, deformities or striped or distorted flowers – they may be suffering from virus diseases, and these will be passed on to the cuttings too.

Also, always avoid taking cuttings from plants that you know to have been affected by pests of any kind, as they may fail to root.

Softwood cuttings – an easy method

One of the most popular and easy methods of propagating greenhouse plants is by softwood cuttings. This is used for such widely grown plants as fuchsias, regal pelargoniums and zonal pelargoniums (or geraniums). It can be done at any time except winter, but spring is best.

Choose a healthy shoot without flowers or flower buds. Cut off a few inches with a sharp knife, cleanly and immediately below a leaf joint.

Gently pull or cut away the lower leaves and any stipules, or 'whiskers'.

Dipping the base of each cutting in hormone rooting powder can hasten rooting and make it more certain, but is by no means essential. Fill a 2½ or 3 in. pot with John Innes seed compost or a compost of equal parts peat and sand. The compost should be moist.

Press the cutting gently into the compost to just below the lowest leaf. If you are taking more than one cutting, several can be put round the side of a slightly larger pot.

Now cover the pot to keep the plant in a moist, warm atmosphere and shade it to prevent loss of moisture through its leaf surfaces.

Special pots with a transparent dome are available for this purpose. Alternatively, ordinary pots or seed trays can be placed in a closed propagating case, or a polythene tent can be constructed over each pot or tray. Do this by inserting bent lengths of wire into the compost, the ends next to the rim of the container, and putting a plastic bag or sheet of polythene over them. Tuck the polythene in under the base. The pots can be put on greenhouse staging but away from strong light.

Cuttings from many easily grown pot plants can also be rooted in polythene bags. Place a little compost at the bottom of the bag, insert the cuttings in this, seal the top of the bag and hang it in a warm place – in a kitchen would be ideal.

With all methods, keep the compost moist by spraying occasionally with a fine mist of water.

Bottom heat is essential for the rooting of some warm greenhouse plants. This is best provided by soil-warming cables in a greenhouse propagator (p. 30).

The formation of top growth is a sign that rooting has occurred. This should take about three weeks. The plants must then be potted on into 3½ in. pots of John Innes No. 1 or 2 compost or a proprietary potting compost (p. 33).

Most young plants from rooted cuttings should not be exposed to direct sunlight even if they are sun lovers. Full light should be given to them only very gradually as their roots develop.

Keep the compost moist, but not wet – waterlogging may prevent formation of roots in many cases, although some plants, such as *Impatiens sultanii* (busy lizzie), will root simply by putting cuttings in a glass of clean water.

1 *At any time except winter cut off a few inches of a healthy shoot without buds or flowers. Cut cleanly, immediately below a leaf joint on the stem*

2 *Gently pull the leaves away from the lower part of the cutting*

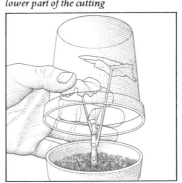

3 *Press the cutting into moist compost, and cover to keep humid*

Leaf cuttings for popular pot plants

Many widely grown pot plants, such as foliage begonias, saintpaulias, streptocarpus, gloxinias and sansevierias, can be propagated from leaf cuttings in various ways.

One method, often successful with begonias, is to pick a leaf and remove the stalk, then carefully cut across the veins in several places.

Fill a seed tray with seed compost and lay the leaves flat on the surface of the compost.

Weigh them down with stones, or peg with bent wire to keep the veins in contact with the soil. Place a sheet of glass or polythene over the tray to retain moisture, and put the covered tray in a warm propagator at a temperature of 18–21°C (64–70°F). After a few weeks, roots should form where the slits were made. Each rooted part can then be separated and potted individually in 3½ in. pots of potting compost. Put them on greenhouse staging, shaded from strong light for a few days.

Another method, used for begonias and peperomias, is to cut the leaves into small triangular sections with a piece of the stalk at the apex of each. The triangles are inserted apex down in the compost, covered and treated as before.

The long leaves of plants such as sansevierias and streptocarpus can be cut into sections about 2 in. long. Each section is inserted vertically in the compost.

The best method for saintpaulias, and other small-leaved plants is to cut off leaves with ½–1 in. of stem.

Insert the stalks individually in a 2½ in. pot, or three in a 3½ in. pot, of seed compost so that the base of each leaf just touches the compost. Cover the containers and place them in warmth. Bottom heat of 16–18°C (61–64°F) will produce rooting in 10–14 days, and new growth should appear above the surface about one month after insertion.

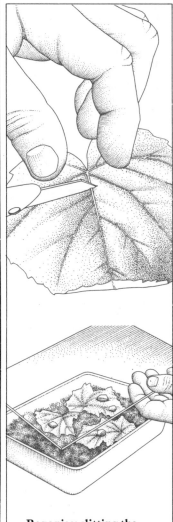

Begonias: slitting the veins *Pick some leaves and remove the stalks. Cut the leaf veins in several places. Lay the leaves flat on seed compost. Place a sheet of glass over the tray and put it in a warm propagator*

Saintpaulias: taking leaves with stems attached *Cut off cleanly the required number of leaves, each with ½–1 in. of stem attached. Insert the stalks in a pot of seed compost so that the base of each leaf just touches the surface. Cover the pot and place it in warmth*

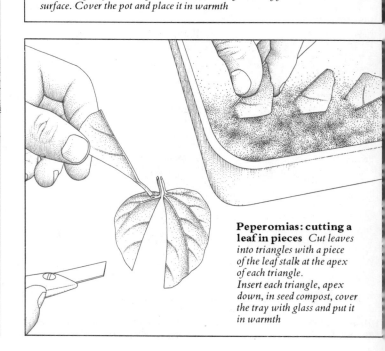

Peperomias: cutting a leaf in pieces *Cut leaves into triangles with a piece of the leaf stalk at the apex of each triangle. Insert each triangle, apex down, in seed compost, cover the tray with glass and put it in warmth*

Mist – for quicker and better results

Intermittent mist propagation is a more expensive but more efficient alternative to keeping cuttings in a closed case or in a bag.

A thin film of moisture is maintained over the leaf surfaces using a water jet controlled automatically by an electronic leaf element or detector unit. This switches itself on only when the cuttings begin to dry.

With this method, propagation can be carried out in full sunlight, and the normal processes involved in plant food formation – known as photosynthesis – can take place.

Bottom heat is usually needed to

A mist unit with surround

balance the cooling effect of moisture passing constantly through the compost and to encourage healing, callus formation and rooting.

With mist propagation rooting is more rapid and certain, and cuttings

that with other methods root with difficulty only or not at all, usually succeed. Also there is usually less disease (particularly grey mould), because spores are washed away before they can do any damage.

The only drawback to mist propagation is that cuttings rooted by this method are more tender than those raised under glass in the ordinary way and need to be hardened off with great care.

Small misting units, with a surround to keep the mist within bounds, can be bought for slightly more than a heated propagator.

Increasing perennial pot plants by division

Division is an easy way of propagating perennial greenhouse plants. It should be done in early spring, before new season's growth begins.

Tap the plant, with its compost, out of its pot. If the compost is dry and difficult to dislodge, water it.

Examine the top of the plant to discover where stems or tufts of growth arise. With a very sharp knife, cut firmly down through the plant between the tufts of growth.

It does not matter if roots are not cut cleanly, but the less damage done to them the better. Old or dead roots, or those that are damaged, can be cut away.

Pot each segment separately in potting compost. Water the plants moderately and keep them in shade for a few days. Most plants will flower the same year.

Many greenhouse bulbs, including hippeastrums, form offsets – small bulbs that sprout from the parent bulb. They can be pulled away during repotting and potted individually in 3–5 in. pots. Use the same compost and the same heat as for the adult plants. It is often necessary to grow these small bulbs for two years or more until they have reached flowering size.

Other methods

Layering is an effective method of propagating some climbing and trailing plants. Bend down a branch so that its stem touches some seed compost placed in a 3–4 in. pot. Slit the stem at this point or peel away a tiny piece of the outer skin. Keep the wound in contact with the compost with a staple made from bent wire, or a weight such as a small stone. When roots have formed, which should usually take between three and six months, cut the stem carefully away from the parent plant. Greenhouse shrubs that do not root easily from cuttings can be propagated by air layering. Exam-

1 *In early spring cut down through the plant between the tufts of growth*

2 *After removing old or dead roots, pot each segment separately*

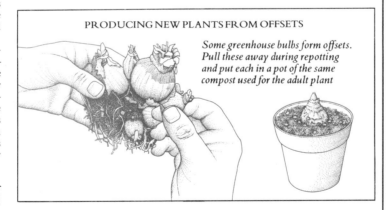

PRODUCING NEW PLANTS FROM OFFSETS

Some greenhouse bulbs form offsets. Pull these away during repotting and put each in a pot of the same compost used for the adult plant

ples are gardenia and stephanotis. Air layering is also used to shorten leggy plants such as the rubber plant, *Ficus elastica*. The method is given in full on page 15.

Sometimes, seed can be saved as a means of propagation. It is no use saving seed from hybrid plants as it cannot be relied on to yield identical plants, but species plants will come true to type. Make sure seed is ripe before collecting, and sow as soon as possible afterwards. The technique is explained on page

36. Popular plants which provide good results from seed are: celosia, eccremocarpus, freesia, *Solanum apsicastrum* and torenia.

Some greenhouse plants, such as *Saxifraga stolonifera*, produce runners with plantlets. These can be pegged down on to compost between spring and autumn in the same way as strawberries.

Passiflora can be propagated by detaching the suckers it throws up, each with some roots attached, and planting them.

Small-scale
greenhouse gardening

Vegetables
and cut flowers

Frames – for small-scale greenhouse gardening

A garden frame consists of a framework of wood, metal, concrete or brick covered by hinged, removable or sliding panes of glass called lights. It can be unheated – known as a cold frame – or heated. Lights can also be bought separately to place on top of existing brick sides or over a pit. A frame enables those without a greenhouse to carry out some greenhouse gardening on a small scale. For a gardener with a greenhouse, it is an essential adjunct.

Aluminium alloy framework is lighter and more durable than wood.

A portable frame is the most convenient type. It can be moved to sunny or shady positions, depending on the plants grown or the time of year, and can be mounted on a low base of bricks or concrete blocks to provide extra light.

A row of frames can be built along one side of a greenhouse that has a brick or concrete base, so that they benefit from its warmth. The frames should be placed on the shadier side of the greenhouse, to avoid excess heat and sunlight. Portable frames can be similarly sited.

To accommodate pot plants, the floor of a frame can be covered with shingle or weathered ash. This prevents worms entering the pots and the compost from becoming soggy, as well as keeping down the weeds.

A cold frame is popularly used to harden off plants raised in the greenhouse, or on a window-sill, before they are planted out in the garden.

It can also be used to raise early crops of low-growing vegetables such as lettuces, radishes and spring onions; thus leaving tomatoes, climbing French beans and other tall plants to make use of the greenhouse height.

Tender biennials such as cineraria, calceolaria, primula and cyclamen can be sown in a cold frame in summer, and kept there in pots through winter before being transferred to the greenhouse staging in the spring. Cuttings of hardy shrubs and perennials taken in summer can be kept in the frame overwinter, before planting out.

The provision of heating by soil-warming cables enlarges the scope of a frame by enabling even earlier vegetables to be grown, and a wider range of plants from seeds.

A frame with air-warming cables is used for overwintering tender plants like fuchsias and pelargoniums, more efficient propagation and growing melons and cucumbers.

Soil-warming and air-warming kits are available for frames, and all that is then needed is for a qualified electrician to provide an outdoor electric supply. A thermostat should be incorporated.

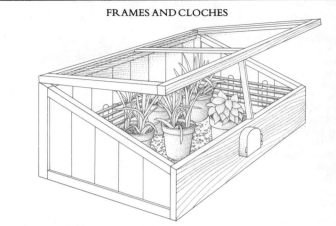

FRAMES AND CLOCHES

Cold frames are used to raise early vegetables, harden off bedding plants raised in the greenhouse and raise plants from cuttings and seeds. Heated frames provide even earlier vegetables and widen the range of plants raised from seeds. They can also house tender plants in winter

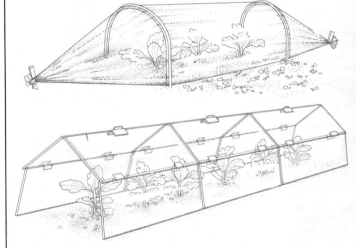

Cloches protect plants, speed up their growth and extend their growing season at both ends. They can also be used to overwinter hardy crops, obtain early strawberries, grow hardy melons and early ridge cucumbers in cold areas, and for propagation. Glass cloches trap more heat, but plastic tunnel cloches are cheap to make from plastic sheeting supported and secured at intervals with double loops of bent wire, one inside the plastic and one outside

Cloches – for vegetables and cut flowers

Cloches are glass or plastic tunnels placed over rows of plants to keep out frost and cold winds. They speed up growth and extend the growing season at both ends, particularly in the vegetable garden.

They should be placed in position to warm the soil about a week before the seeds or plants are put in.

Other uses of cloches include: overwintering hardy crops such as lettuces and carrots; obtaining early

yields of strawberries; and, in colder areas or cool summers, growing early ridge cucumbers.

Hardy melons can also be grown under cloches. Several plants grown for cut flowers – for example, anemones, violets and gladioli – can be advanced or protected under cloches.

Cloches can also be used for the outside rooting of cuttings and the germination of seeds.

Raising bedding plants for the open garden

Many greenhouse plants can be put out in the open garden to flower during summer. This technique, called summer bedding, can be used with plants needing a minimum temperature of up to 16°C (61°F).

Using the greenhouse or a frame to raise summer bedding plants from seeds can save a considerable amount of money each year, and enable you to experiment with new varieties. Raising greenhouse plants from seeds is described on page 36.

In the greenhouse most half-hardy plants can be sown from January to March. Fast-growing plants, such as African marigolds, should not be sown until April: plants sown earlier would be spoilt by being starved in boxes until the temperature was suitable for planting them out – mid to late May, according to the area. Slow-growing plants, such as fibrous begonias, need sowing in January.

Prick out the seedlings into trays or boxes.

Plants that do not like root disturbance, such as zinnias and column stocks, are better pricked straight out into individual small pots and then potted on until ready for planting out.

Some popular bedding plants can be raised from cuttings. Examples are zonal pelargoniums (geraniums), fuchsias, shrubby calceolarias, heliotropes and all chrysanthemums, except annual types.

All plants for bedding out must be hardened off gradually before full exposure to the weather. First put plants in cooler parts of the greenhouse, then transfer them to closed unheated frames. Gradually increase the ventilation of the frames until they are left fully open all the time.

Half-hardy bedding plants should not be planted out until all danger of frost has passed.

Growing climbers and wall shrubs

A few climbing plants or wall shrubs, trained up into the roof on wires, can give a greenhouse an attractively mature appearance in a fairly short time. They also make use of the upper half of the greenhouse, which is often wasted space.

Climbers, and especially wall shrubs, are particularly useful in a lean-to greenhouse where a bare supporting wall can be effectively covered. They also give shade in the summer, partially covering the greenhouse roof so that shade-loving plants can be grown below.

Many climbers and wall shrubs can be planted permanently in the greenhouse border, where they will flower for many years and need little attention apart from an annual top-dressing of well-rotted manure or garden compost, and some cutting back in the autumn.

Ideal for growing in the border are *Abutilon megapotamicum, Bougainvillea glabra, Lapageria rosea, Passiflora caerulea, Plumbago capensis,* and tibouchina.

Some climbers are more suited to growing in pots to contain their growth and, like *Jasminum polyanthum* which flowers in the winter, can be stood outside in summer.

Other climbers suitable for pots include *Cobaea scandens,* dipladenia, gloriosa (glory lily), *Eccremocarpus scaber* and ipomoea (morning glory). They should be planted in 10–12 in. pots of John Innes No. 3, or a peat-based compost.

All the climbers mentioned can be grown in a cool greenhouse where the winter temperature does not drop below 4–7°C (40–45°F).

However, *Abutilon megapotamicum, Jasminum polyanthum,* lapageria and *Passiflora caerulea* can all be grown in a sheltered spot in a cold greenhouse. Additional warmth is not necessary unless the temperature outside drops below –7°C (19°F).

GREENHOUSE CALENDAR

Spring

March
Ventilate, damp down and water as necessary (see February). Some shading may be needed. Pot on over-wintered annuals and established plants that are pot-bound. Congested specimens may be divided.

Sow seeds of half-hardy and tender annuals and perennials. Prick off seedlings from earlier sowings. Complete pruning of climbers.

Begonias, achimenes and other plants with dormant fleshy roots should be started into growth at a temperature of 13–16°C (55–61°F). Hippeastrum (amaryllis) bulbs may be started in gentle warmth. Begin watering when leaves appear.

Prick out tomato seedlings.

Rooted cuttings of late chrysanthemums should be put in a cold frame from the end of the month. Protect with matting if frost is likely.

Pot on and make a first stopping of perpetual carnations. Ventilate freely on warm days.

April
Increase ventilation as the weather gets warmer, and make sure plants do not dry out. Shade the glass during long sunny spells. Damp down the greenhouse regularly during warm periods.

Complete potting up of begonia tubers, gesnerias and other dormant fleshy roots.

Seeds of *Solanum capsicastrum* and *Campanula pyramidalis* should be sown now, at a minimum temperature of 13–16°C (55–61°F).

May
Ventilate freely during the day; damp down and water plants daily, and give special care to shading young plants. Pinch out young plants of fuchsia, plumbago and bouvardia to promote bushy growth. Pot on at regular intervals, so that plants do not get pot-bound and suffer a check.

Put chrysanthemums in their final pots before the end of the month. Support with canes. A week to ten days later, move the pots to a standing ground outside.

Ventilate perpetual carnations freely. Shade lightly. Damp down regularly. Pot on young rooted cuttings. Second-year plants in 6 in. pots should be moved on to 8 in. pots. Make a second stopping.

41

Greenhouse plants/19

Greenhouse calendar

Summer

June
Pay particular attention to watering during hot spells, as well-rooted pot plants can dry out in a few hours. Ventilate freely on warm days, damp down paths and benches once or twice daily. Take softwood cuttings of abutilon, begonia, coleus, fuchsia, pelargonium and tibouchina. Leaf cuttings can be taken of streptocarpus and *Begonia rex*.

Give exhibition incurved and single varieties of chrysanthemums a second stopping about the middle of the month.

July/August
Sow seeds of cineraria early in July and calceolaria from mid-July onwards in cold frames. Softwood and leaf cuttings can still be taken. Water, ventilate and damp down as for June.

In August take cuttings of *Campanula isophylla*. Rest hippeastrum bulbs by reducing watering.

Late chrysanthemums grown for exhibition should have the stems reduced to the strongest two or three to each plant.

Freely ventilate perpetual carnations at all times, and lightly shade on the hottest days. Continue to disbud. Water and feed regularly.

Autumn

September
Continue to ventilate, damp down and water as during the summer, unless the weather turns cold. Reduce feeding towards the end of the month, ceasing it entirely for plants that have finished growing. Bring in young plants of cineraria and calceolaria from cold frames.

Sow cyclamens and annuals for spring flowering under glass. Begin potting spring-flowering bulbs.

Towards the end of the month, bring late-flowering chrysanthemums into the greenhouse. Ventilate freely unless frost is forecast.

Plant tender bulbs such as lachenalia in a cool greenhouse.

October
Cease feeding by the end of the month and remove permanent shading, except over ferns. Ventilate and damp down on warm days, but prepare to turn on heating if cold spells or frosts are forecast.

Thin out overgrown climbers to admit light.

Ventilate chrysanthemums during the day, but a little heat will be needed on frosty nights. Disbud later flowering varieties.

Cuttings of perpetual carnations can be taken from now until March.

November
Ventilate cool and cold greenhouses on sunny days, but shut the ventilators early in the afternoon. Complete potting on of autumn-sown annuals, like salpiglossis, lobelias and schizanthus, for a spring display, and cuttings of pelargoniums, fuchsias and heliotropes.

Several hardy perennials, such as astilbe and polyanthus, will flower during late winter in a cool greenhouse if lifted from the garden now. Pot them but leave them outside.

Maintain a minimum temperature of 7°C (45°F) for perpetual carnations, and ventilate on mild or sunny days. Disbud flowering stems, and feed and water sparingly.

Winter

December
Do any necessary watering and ventilating on mild and sunny days. Remove dead or dying leaves and flowers regularly.

Astilbe and polyanthus plants in pots for early flowering can be brought into a cool greenhouse. Clean the glass so that the weak winter light is not further diffused.

Water stools of late chrysanthemums and increase temperature. Begin taking cuttings towards the end of the month.

Continue to disbud perpetual-flowering carnations; water and feed sparingly. Maintain a minimum temperature of 7°C (45°F).

January
Clean the panes to let in maximum light. Ventilate a cool or cold greenhouse on mild and sunny days. Water sparingly, especially during dull, cold or foggy weather. Remove dead and dying leaves and flowers before they become a source of disease; overwintering cuttings, especially of zonal pelargoniums (geraniums), should be regularly picked over.

Ventilate a warm greenhouse if the temperature exceeds 21°C (70°F) and give it a light damping down.

Take cuttings of late-flowering chrysanthemums. Cuttings taken in December will be ready for potting at the end of the month.

Ventilate perpetual carnations on mild and sunny days. Water and feed sparingly. Cuttings can be taken. Pot rooted cuttings taken earlier. Watch out for aphids and carnation rust.

February
Ventilate cool and cold greenhouses on sunny and mild days; lightly damp down paths and benches with a fine-rosed watering can around midday. Do not over-water plants, but give special attention to mature plants which dry out quickly.

Ventilate a warm greenhouse if the temperature exceeds 21°C (70°F); damp down lightly.

Move dormant plants of heliotrope, fuchsia and bouvardia on to the greenhouse staging and lightly water. Spray over with water each day, and as growth commences increase watering. Maintain a minimum of 7–10°C (45–50°F).

Seeds of half-hardy and tender annuals and perennials, such as tuberous and fibrous begonias, cel- osia, coleus and streptocarpus, can be sown if a minimum temperature of 13–16°C (55–61°F) can be maintained. Sow schizanthus now to provide flowers for late spring and early summer.

Tomatoes for planting out under glass in April should be sown about the middle of the month. They will need a temperature of 16°C (61°F).

At the end of the month, a batch of achimenes may be started into growth. Place the scaly rhizomes about 1 in. apart each way, in moist peat, at a temperature of 13–16°C (55–61°F). When the shoots are about 1–2 in. tall, place four or five together in a 5 in. pot and put it on the greenhouse staging for growing on.

Passiflora and plumbago can be pruned towards the end of the month. Cut back previous season's shoots to within 3 in. from their base.

Pot chrysanthemum cuttings taken in January, and keep all young plants moist.

Ventilate perpetual carnations on mild and sunny days. Water and feed sparingly. Disbud flowering stems as necessary. For indoor use cut the flowers immediately they open. Take more cuttings. Pot those already rooted.

What can go wrong with greenhouse plants

Symptoms	Cause	Cure
Leaves have brown margins and appear scorched or have a bleached appearance. Plants are often checked in growth	Usually a combination of too much heat and lack of shade	Except for most cacti and many succulents, plants under glass should not be allowed to suffer temperatures above 29°C (84°F) without either ventilation or shading, or both. Plants that have suffered excess heat should be shaded and watered sparingly for three to four days. If they are pot-bound, apply a liquid or foliar feed
Flower buds yellow, wither and often drop prematurely; the growing point may also be shrivelled and the leaves somewhat flaccid and lack lustre. The plants are inclined to wilt readily	Persistent under-watering, sometimes as a result of too little space between pot rim and soil level	To give enough room for adequate watering, there should be a gap between soil level and pot rim at least one-tenth of the pot depth. Plants showing symptoms should be watered thoroughly, if necessary by standing them in a bucket of water for several minutes. Subsequently, water normally, making sure that at each watering a little trickles out of the drainage holes
Plants in pots or containers produce thin growth and lack vigour; leaves are small and often yellowish	If no signs of pest or disease present, then probably starvation	Apply a liquid feed, and possibly also a foliar feed, according to maker's instructions. If the container is choked with roots, repot into a larger pot. Plants that respond to division should be divided and potted separately
Leaves and young shoots have a fine powdery white coating, often accompanied by distortion. Later, the powdery areas may take on purplish or reddish hues; the leaves may fall prematurely	Mildew	Fumigate with dinocap smokes or spray with benomyl, dinocap or thiophanate-methyl
Leaves finely mottled and yellowing, eventually shrivelling or falling prematurely; in severe attacks, the shoots are weakened and become covered with a fine webbing	Red spider mites	Spray with derris, malathion or dimethoate
Leaves and petals mottled or with bleached areas	Thrips	Spray or dust with BHC, malathion, nicotine or derris
Young shoots and leaves stunted or malformed; covered in greenish, pink or black insects	Aphids	Spray with derris, malathion, dimethoate or pirimicarb
Leaves often mottled yellow and young shoots less vigorous. When lightly shaken insects like minute white moths take wing	Glasshouse white flies	Spray repeatedly with malathion, BHC or pyrethrum. A difficult pest to eradicate. Fumigate with BHC
The stems and leaf axils are infested with clusters of small insects covered with a waxy white wool. Plant and leaves sometimes yellow and leaves fall early	Mealy bugs	Spray with malathion, nicotine or a systemic insecticide, repeating at regular intervals until the pest has gone. If the attack is slight, wipe off the insects with a soft brush or cloth soaked in soapy water
The plant lacks vigour and looks yellowish, often wilting, even when the soil is moist. When knocked out of pot or dug up, the roots are covered with small soft insects under a waxy whitish wool	Root mealy bugs	Soak root system with malathion, diazinon or nicotine
Stems and leaves bear small, soft, pale brown insects shaped like shields. Plant vigour may be reduced, the leaves yellow and fall prematurely	Scale insects	Spray with malathion, nicotine or a systemic insecticide. If the attack is slight, wipe off the pests with a soft brush or cloth soaked in soapy water
Leaves, and sometimes flowers, become puckered or distorted, the tissues brittle; growing points may die out	Tarsonemid mites	Apply finely powdered sulphur, making sure it gets into leaf axils and growing points
Stems, leaves, flower buds and flowers show brown dead patches of tissue that become covered with a fluffy, greyish-white mould during particularly cool, humid conditions	Botrytis or grey mould	Fumigate with tecnazene smokes or spray with benomyl or thiophanate-methyl
Seedlings, particularly those sown thickly in pots or pans under glass, rot at ground level and topple over	Damping-off disease	Water with quintozene or captan. To prevent this disease, sow seed thinly in a sterilised compost and water in with Cheshunt Compound
Rhododendrons and azaleas in pots show yellow mottled leaves, and may flower poorly	Chlorosis	Repot into an acid compost such as John Innes acid compost or a peat-based compost without lime, and water with clear rain water

Eight of the most popular greenhouse plants

Begonias

Begonia semperflorens

With their beautiful flowers and foliage, the many begonia species and hybrids make excellent greenhouse plants.

Tuberous-rooted begonias The large double-flowered begonias grow from tuberous roots, rather like dahlias. They include the trailing varieties popular for growing in hanging baskets.

Start the tubers into growth in damp peat (p. 36) whenever a minimum of 16°C (61°F) can be maintained. When immersing the tubers in the peat, check that the flat or concave side of each is at the top and just level with the surface.

Inspect the tubers every few days.

As leafy shoots are produced pot them into 3½ in. pots of John Innes No. 2 or similar potting compost. As the roots fill these pots, pot on into 5 in. or 7 in. pots.

Begonia stems and foliage are usually brittle, so tie the stems to a cane at an early stage.

When the plants are well established in their final pots, give regular liquid feeds.

To obtain deep colours, and to keep the greenhouse cool during summer, shade the glass during sunny weather. Larger blooms can be produced by allowing only one shoot to develop from each tuber. Remove the other shoots and use them as cuttings (p. 37). Remove also the female flowers, which have a winged capsule behind the bud and form only single blooms.

Sow begonia seed in January at a temperature of about 16°C (61°F) to get a colourful display the same year. Tubers will be formed and can be saved for subsequent years.

At the end of the year, when the foliage of tuberous begonias begins to yellow, gradually reduce watering until the pots are dry. Turn out the contents of the pots, separate the tubers from adhering compost and store in dry sand in a frost-free place for the winter.

Tuberous-rooted begonias can be put out as summer bedding plants.

The winter-flowering Lorraine varieties are grown from cuttings taken in the spring for flowering the following November at a temperature of 10°C (50°F).

Fibrous-rooted begonias The smaller-flowered *Begonia semperflorens*, popular for bedding out, are grown from seed and have normal, fibrous roots. They are half-hardy perennials often grown as annuals.

They flower well in 3½ in. pots, but the large-flowered forms will do better in 5 in. pots. For the maximum flowering period, sow them in early January at a temperature of 16°C (61°F).

No stopping, staking or tying is necessary. Flowering is prolonged if faded flowers and seed pods are regularly removed.

Foliage begonias The Rex begonias are grown for their leaves, which are patterned in silver, cream, red and purple. *B. masoniana* (iron cross) is another foliage type with bronze-purple markings.

Give foliage begonias humidity and shade in summer. In winter, keep them just moist at a temperature of 13°C (55°F). Pot on in April and increase by division or leaf cutting (p. 38).

Calceolarias

Calceolaria × herbeo-hybrida

Calceolarias have long been favourite greenhouse pot plants. They have exotic pouch-like blooms in a wide range of colours, often with vividly contrasting patterns or spots.

There are large-flowered and many-flowered types. Recently, F1 hybrids have been introduced that are easy to grow and fast flowering.

To grow calceolarias as bedding plants, sow seed in March at 10–13°C (50–55°F). Plant out in the garden at the end of May. Discard plants after flowering.

For Christmas and winter flowering, sow seed in May or June. No artificial warmth is required.

For convenience, seedlings can first be transferred to seed trays, about 20 per tray. Keep the trays in cold frames shaded from direct sunlight. See that the plants do not become dry at any stage, and keep a constant watch for greenfly, to which calceolarias are prone. When the plants are large enough, pot them individually in 5 in. pots, the more compact types in 3½ in. pots. When they begin to show buds, give them regular liquid feeds. The taller varieties will need to be supported with canes.

Bring the plants into the greenhouse in mid-September and overwinter them at 7°C (45°F).

Plants flowering from late winter to early spring need protecting from sudden temperature rises and strong sunlight which will cause wilting. Shade the greenhouse.

During winter, ventilate whenever the weather permits, to lessen the risk of fungus disease attack. Do not use BHC or DDT smokes for controlling pests, since these can blacken calceolarias. Do not spray the plants when in bloom because this can cause rotting of the flowers.

Cinerarias

The daisy-like flowers of cinerarias are borne profusely during half the year in a cool greenhouse – from December to June. They are often richly coloured and sometimes banded with white. Cineraria varieties are divided into the following groups: Hybrida Grandiflora (large broad-petalled flowers); Multiflora Nana (broad-petalled flowers); Stellata (narrow-petalled flowers) and Double-flowered.

Sow and grow cinerarias as described under calceolarias, with this exception: most varieties will need a final 5 in. pot, and large-flowered varieties may require a 7 in. pot. For early and Christmas flowering, sowing should be brought forward earlier than for calceolarias, to about April. Discard the plants after they have flowered.

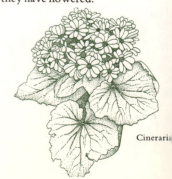

Cineraria

Cyclamens

Cyclamen

Cyclamens are graceful, sometimes sweetly scented plants. The foliage often has beautiful silver markings. Miniature varieties and varieties with frilled flowers and double flowers have been introduced.

Cyclamens react to wide differences in temperature, erratic watering or draughts, by wilting and failing to produce flowers; buds and corms may also rot.

Repot new plants in summer and place the pots in a shady frame. Water lightly until a root system has developed, then begin to water more generously. In late September return the plants to the greenhouse. A temperature of about 13°C (55°F) kept reasonably steady, should be maintained. In districts where low autumn temperatures are likely, put the plants in the greenhouse earlier. Flowering can be expected from winter to spring. Feed and water regularly during late spring and early summer. Later in the summer rest the plants by keeping the compost almost dry, preferably in a shady cold frame.

The following September repot, using the same size container and fresh compost. After some years the corms usually (but not always) begin to produce fewer flowers.

Cyclamens can also be grown from seeds, but buy them from a reliable seedsman. They are large and can be sown individually. Sow them in pots on the surface of any seed compost and cover them with a ¼ in. deep layer of moist peat rubbed through a sieve to remove lumps. The best time for sowing is from August to November. After sowing, place the containers in a propagator where a steady temperature of about 18°C (64°F) can be maintained, to avoid erratic germination. As the seedlings appear above the peat, prick them out promptly into 2½ in. pots of John Innes No. 2 compost.

Retain the seedlings in their initial pots at a temperature of about 18°C (64°F). Keep the compost moist. When the plants are established and making strong growth, lower the temperature to about 16°C (61°F). In April pot on the plants to 5 in. pots and, when the weather is warm enough, transfer them to a shady frame outside.

When potting on at any stage be sure that the top of the corm, however tiny, protrudes above the compost.

In September – or earlier, according to temperature – bring the plants into the greenhouse. Remove premature flower buds to conserve the plants' resources for their major display from December to spring. Give liquid feeds when the flower buds first form.

Corms obtained from seed can be treated in the same way as a bought plant.

Fuchsias

Fuchsia (pendulous)

The fuchsia has many merits. It is relatively easy to grow and has a long flowering season – through summer and autumn. It can be trained to form various shapes and is a good summer bedding plant. Varieties differ widely – some trail or hang, others are erect, some have variegated foliage and *Fuchsia procumbens* has decorative berries.

Buy the plants as rooted cuttings in early spring and pot them in 2½ in. pots of John Innes No. 2 potting compost. Pot on the plants to final 5 in. pots in April or May.

Most fuchsias need some form of training. The simplest is the bush form, which is produced merely by stopping (pinching out) some shoots to induce bushy growth. Rooted cuttings can be stopped when a few inches high to encourage more shoots to rise from the lower parts of the stem.

Trailing plants in hanging baskets also need their growing tips pinched out when the leading shoot is just over the basket edge. Large baskets or hanging containers will need about three plants symmetrically placed in them.

The standard is a beautiful form. In this case, do not remove the growing tip. Encourage the plant to grow a single stem by removing all side-shoots but retaining leaves that spring directly from the stem. As the stem increases in length, tie it to a cane to ensure upright growth. When the desired height has been reached, pinch out the growing tip. As the side-shoots near the top develop, pinch them out when they are a few inches long to encourage more strong growth. Eventually a bushy head will develop.

During the period of active growth remove any weak shoots and give liquid feeds. After pinching out, plants should take six to eight weeks to form flowers as long as they are not stopped again.

Most of the named varieties of greenhouse fuchsias are not hardy and must be kept in a frost-free greenhouse. Give them just enough water in winter to keep the compost slightly moist. In cool conditions some plants may lose their foliage and become dormant, in which case keep them fairly dry. In spring, when new growth appears, begin watering and repotting. When it is seen where new growth comes from, cut away all dead shoots. Unwanted new shoots, removed to develop a shape, can be used for cuttings, which usually root easily (p. 37).

During summer, fuchsias need a cool, moist atmosphere and some ventilation. They should also be slightly shaded. Remove promptly any faded flower heads and their seed pods to ensure the maximum flower production.

Greenhouse plants/23

Eight of the most popular greenhouse plants

Pelargoniums (geraniums)

Regal pelargonium

The most common pelargoniums are zonal pelargoniums, better known as geraniums. Recently, some fine F1 hybrid strains of seeds have been introduced.

Sow zonal pelargoniums as early in the year as possible at a temperature of about 16°C (61°F), for flowering during summer and autumn. After germination transfer the seedlings to small pots and later pot them on into 5 in. pots. Early-sown plants can be used for bedding out.

To obtain winter flowers, take cuttings (p. 37) early in the year from last year's plants retained in the greenhouse. Pot on and during summer sink the pots in soil out of doors in a sunny position; keep the compost moist.

Encourage bushy growth by pinching out the tips of the rooted cuttings when they are a few inches high. Remove any premature flower buds and in autumn take the plants into the greenhouse. With a winter minimum of 10°C (50°F), a dry atmosphere, the minimum of water and as much sunlight as possible, the plants should flower well in winter.

Regal or show pelargoniums are the greenhouse pelargoniums proper. These have a very wide colour range, but flower for a much shorter period than zonals. Regals are best obtained as named varieties from a specialist nursery, but cuttings from existing plants can be taken in early spring or during July and August (p. 37).

Pinch out the growing tips of young plants at an early stage to promote bushy growth. To avoid straggly specimens, cut back old saved plants when they show signs of growth in spring. Use the pieces cut off as further cuttings.

Ivy-leaved pelargoniums are mostly trailing plants. They are ideal for hanging baskets, but can also be trained up trellis or wires on the wall of a lean-to.

They have a long flowering period, like zonals, and should be grown in the same way. They need an initial pinching out to promote branching.

The scented-leaved pelargoniums produce less showy flowers. They include a number of species and varieties named after their leaf scent: nutmeg, lemon, orange, rose. The foliage is attractive and fragrant and they can be kept as evergreen ornamentals.

All these pelargoniums need a moist, but never waterlogged, compost at all times during their growing period. In winter most prefer to be kept rather dry and in a dry atmosphere. Cold and damp can cause root and basal stem rot, and frost is usually fatal to the plants. Ventilate freely in winter whenever weather permits.

All pelargoniums root readily from cuttings taken during spring and summer. Rooted cuttings can be kept growing on over winter with a minimum temperature of about 10°C (50°F).

Regal pelargoniums need some shade under glass, but in general pelargoniums prefer plenty of light. Shading is only necessary to prevent scorching and excessively high temperatures under glass.

Primulas

The vast primula genus includes three popular greenhouse pot plants. *Primula malacoides*, which in spring produces dainty circular tiers of flowers, is raised as a biennial. *P. obconica* is a perennial notable for hardly ever being without flowers. It will flower in its first year if the seeds are sown in January or February. *P. sinensis*, best raised as a biennial, has a thick stem bearing two or three whorls of brightly coloured flowers from late February to March. These last two plants have hairy leaves that can irritate sensitive skins.

Sow *P. malacoides* and *P. sinensis* from May to August. A temperature of only about 10°C (50°F) is necessary for germination. Sow *P. obconica* from January to June at a temperature of about 16°C (61°F). In all cases, prick out into 2½ in. pots. Use John Innes No. 2 compost or a peat-based potting compost. Pot on as required, keeping the plants well shaded and the compost evenly moist. *P. obconica* needs a final 5 or 6 in. pot, the others 4–5 in. Over-winter them at a minimum temperature of about 7°C (45°F).

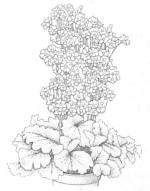

Primula malacoides

Schizanthus

Schizanthus

This dainty annual, which produces masses of colourful flowers, is usually grown as a biennial in the greenhouse, to flower in spring.

Choose giant-flowered varieties such as Sutton's Giant Pansy-Flowered and Sutton's Giant Hybrids. These strains have large, richly coloured flowers usually veined with gold.

Sow in autumn. Pinch out the growing tips of the plants when they are a few inches high and do the same with side-shoots. Do this twice so that good bushy growth develops. By February the plants should be in 5–7 in. pots.

Schizanthus benefit from generous liquid feeding as they grow. Each plant should be tied to a cane.

In winter schizanthus need only frost-free conditions and all the light possible. In summer, shade them to prevent scorching.

To grow schizanthus as an annual use the dwarf compact varieties described in the seed catalogues. 'Dwarf Bouquet' and 'Hit Parade' are especially good. These can be grown without any stopping and will flower well in 3½ in. pots. If preferred, they can be stopped once and potted on to 5 in. pots to make larger plants. Sow in early spring at about 10°C (50°F).

Index

Pictures on pages 2 and 24 by kind permission of the House of Rochford.
Picture on page 16 from Harry Smith Horticultural Photographic Collection.